Information Literacy Toolkit

GRADES 7 and UP

JENNY RYAN

STEPH CAPRA

AMERICAN LIBRARY ASSOCIATION
Chicago and London   2001

Consulting editor, Donald A. Adcock

Cover design by Megan Hibberd, Kean Design, Eight Mile Plains, Q. Australia

The paper used in this publication meets the minimum requirements of American National Standard for Information Sciences—Permanence of Paper for Printed Library Materials, ANSI Z39.48-1992. ∞

Library of Congress Cataloging-in-Publication Data
Ryan, Jenny, 1955-
    Information literacy toolkit. Grades 7 and up / Jenny Ryan and Steph Capra.
       p.   cm.
    Includes bibliographical references and index.
    ISBN 0-8389-3508-7 (alk. paper)
    1. Information literacy—Study and teaching (Secondary)—United States. 2. Information literacy—Study and teaching (Middle school)—United States. 3. Information resources—Evaluation—Study and teaching (Secondary)—United States. 4. Information resources—Evaluation—Study and teaching (Middle school)—United States.   I. Capra, Steph.

ZA3075 .R92 2001
020′∏.71′273—dc21   00-051091

Printed in the United States of America

05   5 4 3

To our ever-supportive families:
the two Petes, Carlie, Dave,
Michelle, Kris, John,
and Leon

Contents

Acknowledgments

Our special thanks to the following for their continuing support, encouragement, and valued professional contribution:

Michelle Young,
St. Rita's Primary School,
Victoria Point

Raylee Elliott-Burns,
Brisbane Catholic Education

Karen Bonanno,
Karen Bonanno & Associates

Robyn Hindmarsh,
Mary MacKillop Catholic
Primary School

Brian Armour,
Redlands College

Jan Barnett,
St. Lawrence's College

Clare Burford,
St. Joseph's, Nudgee

Kerryl Fleming,
John Paul College

Anne Green,
Redeemer Lutheran College

Joan Jenkins,
St. Aidan's School

Maryanne Salisbury,
Runcorn State High School

Fraser-Cooloola District
Technology Group

And to Jamie McKenzie,
whose words of wisdom
and encouragement were
inspirational.

We thank you.

Introduction

Educators of the twenty-first century now face the challenge of preparing learners and workers for the information age. With the societal shift from an industrial model to an information model comes the emphasis on information literacy skills. People must be able to think critically, use learning technologies, and access and use information to participate effectively in society. It is necessary to learn the skills of "learning how to learn" to become lifelong learners.

For many years, academics and researchers have struggled to find a definition for the term "information literacy." While the definitions themselves may vary somewhat, a consistent common thread is the notion that information literacy encompasses critical thinking and problem solving as well as the ethical use of information. We have adopted the definition of information literacy from the "Final Report" of the American Library Association Presidential Committee on Information Literacy:

> To be information literate, a person must be able to recognize when information is needed and have the ability to locate, evaluate, and use effectively the needed information.[1]

In 1998, the American Association of School Libraries (AASL) and the Association for Educational Communications and Technology (AECT) published *Information Power: Building Partnerships for Learning,* which identified the stages of information problem solving as being the key elements of an information literacy curriculum.[2] It also identified the benefits of the library media specialist working collaboratively with teachers to integrate information literacy into the curriculum. This partnership helps facilitate the change from textbook-based learning to resource-based learning—an approach that uses a variety of resources. Resource-based learning is an essential component of an information literacy program that supports the acquisition of lifelong learning skills.

Another book by AASL and AECT, *Information Literacy Standards for Student Learning,* groups the information literacy standards in three broad categories: information literacy, independent learning, and social responsibility.[3] The book provides three levels of proficiency—basic, proficient, and exemplary—to gauge the mastery of each information literacy standard.

It is this holistic approach to information literacy that is crucial to the development of individuals who will contribute positively to society and contribute to the economic development of this country. The emphasis on independent learning culminating in social responsibility may be achieved through a structured-process approach to the teaching of information literacy.

Information Power also acknowledged and supported the integral role of the library media specialist in the development of information literacy in students. As a collaborative partner providing sustained professional input, the library media specialist helps create a rich learning environment.

Integrating information technology skills into the curriculum using the information literacy process outlined in this *Information Literacy Toolkit* is an educationally sound means for students to acquire computer skills. In fact, the International Society for Technology in Education's publication *National Educational Technology: Standards for Students* clearly links the skills of computer literacy to those found in the process overviews in part 1 of the *Toolkit.*[4] Teaching these literacy skills in a cohesive manner is a critical factor in achieving information literacy behaviors in students. Developing these skills to create lifelong learners and socially responsible members of society is the ultimate goal of educators across all curriculum areas. The *Information Literacy Toolkit: Grades Kindergarten–6* was developed to address the issue of supporting educators in teaching lifelong-learning skills. A process approach to teaching these skills forms the basis for the information literacy program.

The Vision

The use of the *Information Literacy Toolkit* provides a powerful model to integrate national and state standards into curriculum planning. It is a focal planning tool for teachers and library media specialists.

Linking information literacy with unit or subject areas, these planning tools integrate information literacy into the curriculum across all subject areas. By using the forms provided when planning curricula, skills can be taught that may have previously been thought difficult to integrate. The structure of the *Toolkit* provides a base on which to build knowledge of information literacy. It is crucial to include the entire six-stage process rather than individual skills because each skill forms part of the total process. Students need to achieve a high degree of understanding that it is this process approach to learning that provides them with behaviors for lifelong learning.

The *Information Literacy Toolkit* facilitates curriculum planning. With the accompanying CD-ROM, the *Toolkit* forms the basis on which to create a comprehensive, cohesive, and sequentially developed school-based information literacy program.

The *Toolkit* has three major components:

1. process overviews with a scope and sequence listing of the progressive skills for each of the six stages of the process

2. planning organizers for use when determining the year's curriculum units

3. teaching tools to draw from for information literacy process activities applicable to the units of study

Information literacy is a six-stage process. The flexible structure of the process makes it applicable as a planning tool for any process approach to teaching information literacy, e.g., Big6, etc.

Links from *Information Literacy Standards for Student Learning* to the *Toolkit*

As stated previously, AASL's *Information Literacy Standards for Student Learning* provides national guidelines for information literacy and identifies three categories of learning—information literacy, independent learning, and social responsibility. The *Toolkit* skills found in part 1, "Process Overviews," articulate a sequential and developmental program that encompasses AASL's standards in a flexible teacher-planning format. The nine standards follow.

Information Literacy

Standard 1: The student who is information literate accesses information efficiently and effectively.

Standard 2: The student who is information literate evaluates information critically and competently.

Standard 3: The student who is information literate uses information accurately and creatively.

Independent Learning

Standard 4: The student who is an independent learner is information literate and pursues information related to personal interests.

Standard 5: The student who is an independent learner is information literate and appreciates literature and other creative expressions of information.

Standard 6: The student who is an independent learner is information literate and strives for excellence in information seeking and knowledge generation.

Social Responsibility

Standard 7: The student who contributes positively to the learning community and to society is information literate and recognizes the importance of information to a democratic society.

Standard 8: The student who contributes positively to the learning community and to society is information literate and practices ethical behavior in regard to information and information technology.

Standard 9: The student who contributes positively to the learning community and to society is information literate and participates effectively in groups to pursue and generate information.[5]

The skills identified in the *Toolkit* will assist in the development of students as socially responsible members of society. By using a process approach, students have the opportunity to practice the skills of

- critical thinking and problem solving
- being socially responsible participants within society

The ability to solve problems will prepare students for an information-based society and a workplace centered on technology. To develop skills in problem solving and to overcome the problem of plagiarism, students must be given the opportunity to offer original solutions to a problem. By framing a unit of work as a problem or task, rather than a topic, students have the opportunity to create and present original ideas as opposed to simply reading and regurgitating the knowledge of others.

Sequentially developed skills provide opportunities for students to acquire attitudes and behaviors relating to the ethical use of information. The infor-mation literacy program provides sustained opportunities for students to become socially responsible, active participants in society.

The School-Wide Initiative

A whole-school approach to integrating information literacy across grades K–12 will result in students' exposure to a comprehensive development of skills and competency in the use of a process approach to problem solving. The CD-ROM that accompanies the *Toolkit* can be used to create a whole-school document.

You can achieve maximum staff ownership if staff cooperatively complete and modify their own planning documents. Subsequent whole-staff discussion and modification of the resulting planners, commencing with the lowest level and progressing to the highest, enable teachers to understand the sequential and developmental nature of the information literacy program.

The process of adapting the program will be ongoing to meet changing curriculum needs. It may take schools up to twelve months using and modifying the initial planning organizers to reflect the elements of the school's requirements. All skills, particularly those of computer literacy, will require adaptation to school circumstances.

How to Use the *Toolkit*

Part 1 of the *Toolkit* defines the six stages of the information literacy process and shows the progression of skills for each stage across grade levels. It is recommended that all teachers and library media specialists be given a copy of this part and read through it to develop an awareness of the scope and progression of the information literacy skills. If necessary, adjustments can be made to the level of difficulty of skills for a grade level; however, make sure that the integrity of the sequential and developmental nature of the skills is retained. Through this effort it is possible to see what has come before and what the present skills lead to at the next level, giving an overview of the entire process.

Part 2 pulls the skills together for individual grades. Use the planning organizers at the beginning of the school year to map out the units of the curriculum for the year and to connect the information literacy skills to that curriculum. If at all possible, this should be a collaborative effort by teachers and library media specialists so that information literacy can be sequentially integrated into learning activities and assessment tasks. With systematic planning, all skills are covered for each grade level.

Part 3 includes a variety of teaching tools that are applicable across grades and curriculum units. The unit planner found in this part helps you organize the skills, activities, assessment measures, and resources wanted for use with a unit. The introduction provides guidance for framing units as problems to be solved or tasks to be accomplished. It also offers examples of ways to embed technology into the information literacy process.

The planning organizers in part 2 and teaching tools in part 3 of the *Information Literacy Toolkit* may be photocopied for use within a school. These forms are protected by copyright. The publisher and author grant *Information Literacy Toolkit* users the right to reproduce the forms, whether copied as-is or adapted for nonprofit purposes within a single school setting on the condition that the publisher's source line appears on each page. The standard source line included on the documents provided in the book is

> From *Information Literacy Toolkit,* published by the American Library Association. Copyright 2001 by Jenny Ryan and Steph Capra. All rights reserved except those which may be granted by Sections 107 and 108 of the Copyright Revision Act of 1976.

The documents in parts 1 and 2 were prepared in Microsoft Excel 97. For convenience in customizing the files to individual school settings, those files are provided on the CD-ROM at the back of the book. Users who are supplementing these documents with their own material may use the source line:

> Adapted from *Information Literacy Toolkit* (American Library Association, 2001). Copyright 2001 by Jenny Ryan and Steph Capra.

NOTES

1. American Library Assn. Presidential Committee on Information Literacy, "Final Report" (Chicago: American Library Assn., 1989), 1. Available: http://www.ala.org/acrl/nili/ilit1st.html

2. American Assn. of School Librarians and Assn. for Educational Communications and Technology, *Information Power: Building Partnerships for Learning* (Chicago: American Library Assn., 1998).

3. American Assn. of School Librarians and Assn. for Educational Communications and Technology, *Information Literacy Standards for Student Learning* (Chicago: American Library Assn., 1998), 8–9.

4. International Society for Technology in Education, *National Educational Technology Standards for Students* (Eugene, Ore.: The Society, 1998).

5. American Assn. of School Librarians and Assn. for Educational Communications and Technology, *Information Literacy Standards,* 8–9.

Process Overviews

The overviews for each stage of the information literacy process give a broad view of the progression of skills from the lowest to highest degree of competency. The six stages of the process are defined in the following statements to ensure a common understanding. Other terms can be substituted if you are using another process model, while keeping the integrity of the actual process.

1. *Defining* The student formulates questions and analyzes and clarifies the requirements of the problem or task. This is the first stage in the information literacy cycle. As a result of new learnings and understandings, this stage is constantly revisited during the entire process to refine and redefine the problem or task for further clarification.

2. *Locating* The student identifies potential sources of information and locates and accesses a variety of resources using multiple formats.

3. *Selecting/analyzing* The student analyzes, selects, and rejects information from the located resources appropriate to the problem or task.

4. *Organizing/synthesizing* The student critically analyzes and organizes the gathered information, synthesizes new learnings incorporating prior knowledge, and develops original solutions to a problem or task.

5. *Creating/presenting* The student creates an original response to the problem or task and presents the solution to an appropriate audience.

6. *Evaluating* The student critically evaluates the effectiveness of his or her ability to complete the requirements of the task and identifies future learning needs.

The skills contained in each stage of the overview have been extensively benchmarked and validated against national and international standards. Attainment levels for each student continue at an individual rate within a range but generally approximate the relevant year level.

Each new skill, whether a first introduction or an incrementally harder skill, is shown in **bold** in the overviews. Skills already experienced at the same level of complexity as the previous level are shown in regular type.

Within the stages, each skill progresses with decreasing levels of teaching support. The terminology reflects the level of teaching support required:

- "Modeled examples/techniques" is used when a skill is first introduced and has a high level of teacher input and support and the skill is specifically taught.
- "With guidance" reflects the second level of support in which the teacher maintains accessible support for the student—the teacher is the "guide on the side."
- Skills without qualifiers indicate that students are assumed to have competency in this skill, so there is little or no need for direct teacher support.

Give a full set of the process overviews along with the planning organizers to each teacher at the beginning of the academic year. This facilitates the teacher's understanding of the sequential and developmental nature of the skills and this is especially important in ensuring the continuity of the teaching of information literacy in the school.

Information Literacy Planning Organizer 7–12
Overview of Defining Stage

Grade 7. Through planned learning activities the student:

develops appropriate questioning techniques through extensive modeling to clarify requirements of task

selects from a range of topics using modeled techniques

draws on prior knowledge to brainstorm and cluster ideas

identifies and interprets key words in task using modeled techniques

develops focus questions using modeled techniques

devises a time-management strategy to meet given deadlines using modeled techniques

selects an appropriate strategy using modeled examples to record headings and subheadings

makes predictions using models provided about likely sources of information onto search strategy sheet

clarifies and refines research questions using modeled techniques

re-defines problem with guidance when alternative solutions are exhausted

formulates a basic hypothesis using modeled techniques

Grade 8. Through planned learning activities the student:

develops appropriate questioning techniques through extensive modeling to clarify requirements of task

analyzes and clarifies a given task using modeled techniques

selects from a range of topics using modeled techniques

draws on prior knowledge to brainstorm and cluster ideas with teachers and peers

identifies and interprets key words in task using modeled techniques

develops focus questions using modeled techniques

devises a time-management strategy to meet given deadlines using modeled techniques

selects an appropriate strategy using modeled examples to record headings and subheadings

makes predictions using models provided about likely sources of information onto search strategy sheet

clarifies and refines research questions using modeled techniques

re-defines problem with guidance when alternative solutions are exhausted

formulates a basic hypothesis using modeled techniques

Grade 9. Through planned learning activities the student:

consolidates appropriate questioning techniques with guidance to clarify requirements of task

selects from a range of topics with guidance

draws on prior knowledge to brainstorm and cluster ideas

identifies and interprets key words in task with guidance

develops focus questions with guidance

devises a time-management strategy with guidance to meet given deadlines

selects an appropriate strategy with guidance to record headings and subheadings

makes predictions with guidance about likely sources of information onto search strategy sheet

clarifies and refines research questions with guidance

uses reference sources to clarify the meaning of a research task

re-defines problem with guidance when alternative solutions are exhausted

formulates a basic hypothesis with guidance

Grade 10. Through planned learning activities the student:

refines appropriate questioning techniques with guidance to clarify requirements of task

selects from a range of topics

draws on prior knowledge to brainstorm and cluster ideas

identifies and interprets key words in task

develops focus questions with guidance

devises a time-management strategy to meet given deadlines

selects an appropriate strategy to record headings and subheadings

makes predictions with guidance about likely sources of information onto search strategy sheet

clarifies and refines research questions with guidance

uses reference sources to clarify the meaning of a research task

re-defines problem with assistance when alternative solutions are exhausted

negotiates and justifies alternative tasks as appropriate

formulates a hypothesis with guidance

Grade 11. Through planned learning activities the student:

refines appropriate questioning techniques to clarify requirements of task

selects from a range of topics

draws on prior knowledge to brainstorm and cluster ideas

identifies and interprets key words in task

develops questions and responds to a task with guidance which may require:
   identification of trends, analysis, critical evaluation, survey, cause and effect

devises a time-management strategy to meet given deadlines

selects an appropriate strategy to record headings and subheadings

makes predictions about likely sources of information onto search strategy sheet

clarifies and refines research questions

uses reference sources to explore a topic and identify issues and subtopics with guidance

re-defines problem when alternative solutions are exhausted

negotiates and justifies alternative tasks as appropriate

formulates a hypothesis

Grade 12. Through planned learning activities the student:

refines appropriate questioning techniques to clarify requirements of task

selects from a range of topics

draws on prior knowledge to brainstorm and cluster ideas

identifies and interprets key words in task

develops focus questions and responds to a task which may require identification of trends, analysis, critical evaluation,
   survey, cause and effect

devises a time-management strategy to meet given deadlines

selects an appropriate strategy to record headings and subheadings

makes predictions about likely sources of information onto search strategy sheet

clarifies and refines research questions

uses reference sources to explore a topic and identify issues and subtopics

re-defines problem when alternative solutions are exhausted

negotiates and justifies alternative tasks as appropriate

formulates a hypothesis

Information Literacy Planning Organizer 7–12
Overview of Locating Stage

Grade 7. Through planned learning activities the student:

follows a search plan using key words and related terms, modifying where necessary

determines the type of resource most appropriate for the topic

identifies and locates print and non-print resources including:

    understanding organization of resources in school and local libraries

    recognizing the value of fiction for specific topics, e.g., historical fiction

    becoming familiar with limited number of appropriate search engines using modeled techniques

    using simple and combined terms to search catalog, Net and CD-ROM sources

    choosing broader or narrower terms to refine search results

    using Help function to locate information and refine searches

    searching for information using given Internet addresses and managing bookmarks

    using information from the wider community

identifies appropriate resources by:

    using skimming and scanning techniques to survey readability in electronic and print resources

    using contents, index and text headings for all types of resources including electronic

recognizes where currency of information is necessary

recognizes the need to locate a variety of resources representing a range of views

with guidance, extends use of Internet/e-mail by:

    using given Internet addresses with assistance

    bookmarking a location

    composing and sending e-mail

    accessing and reading e-mail

    replying to an e-mail message

    forwarding an e-mail message

    copying/pasting from Web page to document

    being aware of Internet search engines as a source of information

    being aware of Web page structure

extends use of computer system skills using modeled examples by:

    deleting, copying and moving files

    loading software for information retrieval

    selectively printing information from electronic sources under teacher supervision

identifies and locates information from both primary and secondary sources using modeled techniques

uses special print and non-print reference resources using modeled examples

recognizes difference in purpose of magazines, newspapers, pamphlets using modeled techniques

uses range of equipment to access information, e.g., telephone, fax, computer, scanner, digital camera using modeled techniques

uses e-mail to discuss topics and to facilitate cooperative activities using modeled examples

Information Literacy Planning Organizer 7–12
Overview of Locating Stage

Grade 8. Through planned learning activities the student:

identifies and locates text and nontext resources including:

    understanding organization of resources in school and local libraries

    recognizing the value of fiction for specific topics, e.g., historical fiction

    using information from the wider community

    accessing periodical indexes using modeled techniques

extends use of Internet/e-mail with guidance by:

    becoming familiar with limited number of appropriate search engines using modeled techniques

    composing and sending e-mail

    accessing and reading e-mail

    replying to and forwarding an e-mail message

    using e-mail to discuss topics and to facilitate cooperative activities using modeled examples

    searching for information using given URLs and managing bookmarks

    copying/pasting from Web page to document

extends the use of databases with guidance by:

    using simple and Boolean terms to search catalog, Net and CD-ROM sources

    choosing broader or narrower terms to refine search results

    using Help function to locate information and refine searches

recognizes where currency of information is necessary

recognizes the need to locate a variety of resources representing a range of views

identifies and locates information from both primary and secondary sources using modeled techniques

uses special print and non-print reference resources using modeled examples

recognizes difference in purpose of magazines, newspapers, pamphlets using modeled techniques

uses range of equipment to access information, e.g., telephone, fax, computer, scanner, digital camera using modeled techniques

extends use of computer systems skills using modeled examples by:

    deleting, copying and moving files

    loading software for information retrieval

    selectively printing information from electronic sources

Grade 9. Through planned learning activities the student:

identifies and locates text and nontext resources including:

    understanding organization of resources in school and local libraries

    recognizing the value of fiction for specific topics, e.g., historical fiction

    accessing periodical indexes with guidance

extends the use of Internet/e-mail by:

    becoming familiar with limited number of appropriate search engines with guidance

    using e-mail with guidance to discuss topics and to facilitate cooperative activities

    using e-mail to access experts in the field

    searching for information using given URLs and managing bookmarks

extends the use of databases with guidance by:

    using simple and Boolean terms to search catalog, Net and CD-ROM sources

    choosing broader or narrower terms to refine search results

    using Help function to locate information and refine searches

extends use of computer systems skills with guidance by:

    deleting, copying and moving files

    selectively printing information from electronic sources

accesses community and government information sources

recognizes where currency of information is necessary

recognizes the need to locate a variety of resources representing a range of views

identifies and locates information from both primary and secondary sources with guidance

uses special print and non-print reference resources with guidance

recognizes difference in purpose of magazines, newspapers, pamphlets with guidance

uses range of equipment to access information, e.g., telephone, fax, computer, scanner, digital camera

Information Literacy Planning Organizer 7–12
Overview of Locating Stage

Grade 10. Through planned learning activities the student:

identifies and locates text and nontext resources including:

    understanding organization of resources in school, local and state libraries

    recognizing the significance of cross-references and subtopics in an index

extends the use of Internet/e-mail by:

    becoming familiar with a variety of appropriate search engines

    using e-mail to discuss topics and to facilitate cooperative activities

    using e-mail to access experts in the field

    searching for information using given URLs and managing bookmarks

views, downloads and decompresses files from Internet sites with guidance

observes netiquette conventions

extends the use of databases by:

    using simple and Boolean terms to search catalog, Net and CD-ROM sources

    choosing broader or narrower terms to refine search results

    using Help function to locate information and refine searches

uses electronic indexes using modeled examples to locate current information

extends the use of computer systems skills by:

    deleting, copying and moving files

    selectively printing information from electronic sources

accesses community and government information sources

recognizes where currency of information is necessary

recognizes the need to locate a variety of resources representing a range of views

identifies and locates information from both primary and secondary sources

recognizes difference in purpose of magazines, newspapers, pamphlets

uses special print and non-print reference resources

recognizes the "positioning" of the reader by the author

uses range of equipment to access information, e.g., telephone, fax, computer, scanner, digital camera

Grade 11. Through planned learning activities the student:

accesses all types of text and information technologies, including:

    understanding organization of resources in school, local and state libraries

    surveying all aspects of a resource and recognizing the significance of cross-references and subtopics

    searching appropriate databases within the school and wider community

    using advanced search techniques to refine search results

    using e-mail to access experts in the field

uses e-mail to discuss topics and to facilitate cooperative activities

selectively prints information from electronic sources

uses electronic indexes with guidance to locate current information

accesses community and government information sources

recognizes where currency of information is necessary

recognizes the need to locate a variety of resources representing a range of views

identifies and locates information from both primary and secondary sources

recognizes difference in purpose of magazines, newspapers, pamphlets

uses knowledge of coverage and purpose of resources to refine the scope of the search

recognizes the "positioning" of the reader by the author

uses special print and non-print reference resources

uses range of equipment to access information, e.g., telephone, fax, computer, scanner, digital camera

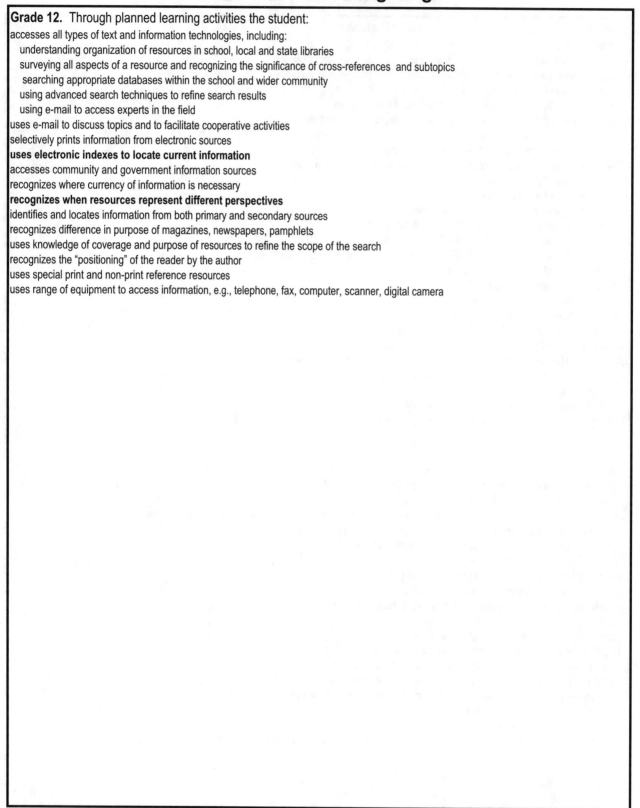

Grade 12. Through planned learning activities the student:

accesses all types of text and information technologies, including:

    understanding organization of resources in school, local and state libraries

    surveying all aspects of a resource and recognizing the significance of cross-references and subtopics

    searching appropriate databases within the school and wider community

    using advanced search techniques to refine search results

    using e-mail to access experts in the field

uses e-mail to discuss topics and to facilitate cooperative activities

selectively prints information from electronic sources

uses electronic indexes to locate current information

accesses community and government information sources

recognizes where currency of information is necessary

recognizes when resources represent different perspectives

identifies and locates information from both primary and secondary sources

recognizes difference in purpose of magazines, newspapers, pamphlets

uses knowledge of coverage and purpose of resources to refine the scope of the search

recognizes the "positioning" of the reader by the author

uses special print and non-print reference resources

uses range of equipment to access information, e.g., telephone, fax, computer, scanner, digital camera

Grade 7. Through planned learning activities the student:

selects resources using modeled techniques by:
  skimming and scanning
  using contents, index and text headings
evaluates appropriateness of resources, discarding if necessary
modifies focus questions using modeled techniques
devises appropriate note-taking templates using modeled examples
records information using modeled examples by:
  using a note-making strategy appropriate to source and problem, e.g., Concept mapping, Outline
  clustering electronic notes under subheadings
  using a clipboard
  selecting appropriate graphic organizer
makes comparisons between the purpose of different writing styles using modeled examples, e.g.,
  Information Report, Persuasive Essay, etc.
compares information from different sources for opposing viewpoints and accuracy using modeled techniques
recognizes the need for adequate data before drawing conclusions
downloads text files from Internet sites using modeled techniques
records bibliographic sources of information using author, title, publisher, date, http, date of download using modeled examples
understands and complies with copyright requirements using modeled examples
observes netiquette conventions when communicating electronically using modeled techniques
understands there may be various interpretations of data
uses a variety of primary and secondary sources using modeled examples

Grade 8. Through planned learning activities the student:

selects resources using modeled techniques by:
  skimming and scanning
  using contents, index and text headings
evaluates appropriateness of resources, discarding if necessary
modifies focus questions using modeled techniques
devises appropriate note-taking templates using modeled examples
records information using modeled examples by:
  using a note-making strategy appropriate to source and problem, e.g., Concept mapping, Outline
  recognizing when a note-making format requires modification
  clustering electronic notes under subheadings
  selecting appropriate graphic organizer
makes comparisons between **different text types using modeled examples, e.g., Information Report, Persuasive Essay, etc.**
compares information from different sources for opposing viewpoints and accuracy using modeled techniques
records bibliographic sources of information using author, title, publisher, date, http, date of download using modeled examples
understands and complies with copyright requirements using modeled examples
downloads text files from Internet sites using modeled techniques
observes netiquette conventions when communicating electronically using modeled techniques
understands there may be various interpretations of data
uses a variety of primary and secondary sources using modeled examples

Information Literacy Planning Organizer 7–12
Overview of Selecting/Analyzing Stage

Grade 9. Through planned learning activities the student:

selects resources with guidance by:
  skimming and scanning
  using contents, index and text headings
analyzes appropriate information using modeled techniques from a variety of sources, including exhibitions, excursions, audio and visual recordings and interviews by:
  using text/context clues such as text headings and subheadings
  identifying main and subordinate ideas
  re-reading, re-listening and re-viewing
evaluates appropriateness of resources, discarding if necessary
modifies focus questions with guidance
devises appropriate note-taking templates with guidance
records information with guidance by:
  devising note-making strategies to ensure information is collected consistently and accurately
  modifying note-making formats as appropriate to the task and information source
  clustering notes under subheadings
  selecting appropriate graphic organizer
makes comparisons with guidance between different text types, e.g., Information Report, Persuasive Essay, etc.
compares information from different sources for opposing viewpoints and accuracy with guidance
records bibliographic sources of information using author, title, publisher, date, http, date of download with guidance
understands and complies with copyright requirements with guidance
downloads text and graphic files from Internet sites with guidance
observes netiquette conventions with guidance
considers a range of viewpoints by:
  recognizing when the information is fact or opinion
  identifying authority, purpose and intended audience of source
  identifying bias and omission in information sources
uses a variety of primary and secondary sources with guidance
understands strategies that may be used to slant information in subtle ways using modeled techniques
using prior knowledge proposes problem-solving strategies for real-life situations

Grade 10. Through planned learning activities the student:

analyzes appropriate information from a variety of sources, including exhibitions, excursions, audio and visual recordings and interviews by:
  using text/context clues such as text headings and subheadings
  identifying main and subordinate ideas
  re-reading, re-listening and re-viewing
evaluates appropriateness of resources, discarding if necessary
modifies focus questions
devises appropriate note-taking templates
records information by:
  devising note-making strategies to ensure information is collected consistently and accurately
  modifying note-making formats as appropriate to the task and information source
  clustering notes under subheadings
  selecting appropriate graphic organizer
makes comparisons between different text types, e.g., Information Report, Persuasive Essay, etc.
compares information from different sources for opposing viewpoints and accuracy
analyzes information deficiencies and locates additional information
records bibliographic sources of information using author, title, publisher, date, http, date of download
understands and complies with copyright requirements
views, downloads and decompresses files from Internet sites with guidance

Grade 10 [cont].

observes netiquette conventions

considers a range of viewpoints by:

    recognizing when the information is fact or opinion

    identifying authority, purpose and intended audience of resource

analyzes statistical data using modeled techniques

uses a variety of primary and secondary sources

identifies strategies used to slant information in subtle ways

using prior knowledge and new learnings, proposes problem-solving strategies for real-life situations

Grade 11. Through planned learning activities the student:

interprets, compares and selects information with guidance after:

    evaluating information for accuracy, bias and omission

    evaluating an argument for logic

    examining reasons for value judgments

    examining reasons for contradictions or seeming contradictions in evidence

devises appropriate note-taking templates

records information by:

    devising note-making strategies to ensure information is collected consistently and accurately

    modifying note-making formats as appropriate to the task and information source

understands and complies with copyright requirements

views, downloads and decompresses files from Internet sites

observes netiquette conventions

analyzes statistical data with guidance

uses a variety of primary and secondary sources

using prior knowledge proposes problem-solving strategies for real-life situations

records bibliographic source using a recognized system of notation

Grade 12. Through planned learning activities the student:

interprets, compares and selects information after:

    evaluating information for accuracy, bias and omission

    evaluating an argument for logic

    examining reasons for value judgments

    examining reasons for contradictions or seeming contradictions in evidence

devises appropriate note-taking templates

records information by:

    devising note-making strategies to ensure information is collected consistently and accurately

    modifying note-making formats as appropriate to the task and information source

understands and complies with copyright requirements

views, downloads and decompresses files from Internet sites

observes netiquette conventions

analyzes statistical data

uses a variety of primary and secondary sources

using prior knowledge proposes problem-solving strategies for real-life situations

records bibliographic source

correctly uses footnotes or endnotes

Information Literacy Planning Organizer 7–12
Overview of Organizing/Synthesizing Stage

Grade 7. Through planned learning activities the student:

synthesizes selected information connecting similar ideas and begins to predict possible outcomes

engages in reflective thinking to analyze and clarify a problem

engages in group discussion to analyze and clarify a problem

is aware there may be alternative solutions to a problem

proposes a solution to a set problem based on prior knowledge and new information which:

   organizes ideas and information logically

   makes simple generalizations and draws simple conclusions

verifies results of experiments using modeled examples

categorizes information according to a framework of headings and subheadings using modeled examples

consolidates the use of word processing skills by:

   selectively cutting and pasting information from an electronic source with guidance

   making notes using word processor or other software to quote a source or make notes

   making notes directly from screen

   using keyboard drills, Spelling, Grammar Check, Undo, Select all, Page Setup

   using lists/bullets

   creating and inserting simple tables

   wrapping text around graphics

   formatting text appropriate to text type

creates computer-generated organizational strategies, e.g., flow charts, time lines using modeled examples

makes notes using modeled techniques, e.g., written bulleted points, note-taking template, clipboards, etc.

extends the use of databases with guidance by:

   browsing, editing and adding records in a class-created database

   sorting and deleting records

   using Find function to search for specific criteria

consolidates the use of spreadsheets by:

   changing column width, row height and alignment

   using simple formulas for basic operations—multiply, subtract and divide

develops the ability to have faith in own judgment and point of view

recognizes information deficiencies and locates additional information

Grade 8. Through planned learning activities the student:

synthesizes information from a variety of sources using modeled examples

combines selected information connecting similar ideas and begins to predict possible outcomes

is aware of alternative consequences of solutions to a problem

proposes a solution to a set problem based on prior knowledge and new information which:

   organizes ideas and information logically

   makes simple generalizations and draws simple conclusions

verifies results of experiments through modeled examples

categorizes information according to a framework of headings and subheadings using modeled examples

consolidates the use of word processing skills by:

   selectively cutting and pasting information from an electronic source with guidance

   making notes using word processor or other software to quote a source or make notes

   making notes directly from screen

   using keyboard drills, Spelling, Grammar Check, Undo, Select all, Page Setup

   using lists/bullets

   creating and inserting simple tables

   wrapping text around graphics

   formatting text appropriate to writing styles

creates computer-generated organizational strategies, e.g., flow charts, time lines using modeled examples

makes notes using modeled techniques, e.g., written bulleted points, note-taking template, clipboards, etc.

Grade 8 [cont].

extends the use of databases with guidance by:
  browsing, editing and adding records in a class-created database
  sorting and deleting records
  using Find function to search for specific criteria
consolidates the use of spreadsheets by:
  changing column width, row height and alignment
  using simple formulas for basic operations—add, multiply, subtract and divide
develops the ability to have faith in own judgment and point of view
recognizes information deficiencies and locates additional information

Grade 9. Through planned learning activities the student:

combines selected information connecting similar ideas
draws inferences from evidence with guidance
synthesizes information to predict consequences and to construct generalizations with guidance
proposes a solution to a set problem based on prior knowledge and new information which:
  organize ideas and information logically
  make simple generalizations and draw simple conclusions
verifies results of experiments with guidance
categorizes information according to a framework of headings, subheadings or database fields with guidance
consolidates the use of word processing skills by:
  selectively cutting and pasting information from an electronic source with guidance
  making notes using word processor or other software to quote a source or make notes
  making notes directly from screen
  using Spelling, Grammar Check, Undo, Select all, Page Setup
  using lists/bullets
  creating and inserting simple tables
  wrapping text around graphics
  formatting text appropriate to writing styles
creates computer-generated organizational strategies with guidance, e.g., flow charts, time lines
makes notes with guidance, e.g., written bulleted points, note-taking template, clipboards, etc.
extends the use of databases with guidance by:
  browsing, editing and adding records in a database
  sorting and deleting records
  using Find function to search for specific criteria
consolidates the use of spreadsheets by:
  changing column width, row height and alignment
  using simple formulas for basic operations—add, multiply, subtract and divide
responds appropriately to the given writing styles, e.g., argument, report, etc.
identifies positive and negative influences in information sources with guidance
recognizes information deficiencies and locates additional information

Information Literacy Planning Organizer 7–12
Overview of Organizing/Synthesizing Stage

Grade 10. Through planned learning activities the student:

combines selected information connecting similar ideas

draws inferences from evidence

synthesizes information to predict consequences and to construct generalizations with guidance

proposes a solution to a set problem based on prior knowledge and new information which:

    organize ideas and information logically

    make generalizations and draw conclusions

verifies results of experiments with guidance

categorizes information according to a framework of headings, subheadings or database fields

consolidates the use of word processing skills by:

    creating computer-generated organizational strategies with guidance, e.g., flow charts, time lines

    making notes, e.g., written bulleted points, note-taking template, clipboards, etc.

extends the use of databases with guidance by:

    browsing, editing and adding records in a database

    sorting and deleting records

    using Find function to search for specific criteria

consolidates the use of spreadsheets by:

    changing column width, row height and alignment

    using simple formulas for basic operations—add, multiply, subtract and divide

responds appropriately to the given text type, e.g., Information Report, Persuasive Essay

identifies positive and negative influences in information sources

recognizes information deficiencies and locates additional information

Grade 11. Through planned learning activities the student:

tests hypotheses statistically using modeled examples

combines selected information connecting similar ideas

synthesizes information, makes generalizations, builds arguments and applies problem-solving strategies

makes inferences and deductions and critiques solutions

verifies results of experiments

categorizes information according to a framework of headings, subheadings or database fields

refines use of appropriate writing styles

evaluates different perspectives and formulates own opinion

applies ethical principles to the use of electronic note-taking

uses appropriate note-taking strategies, e.g., written bulleted points, computer-generated note-taking, clipboards, etc.

gathers specific additional information to support a hypothesis or problem-solving task

refines word processing, spreadsheet and database skills to organize information and create new ideas

consolidates use of computer-generated organizational strategies

Grade 12. Through planned learning activities the student:

tests hypotheses statistically

combines selected information connecting similar ideas

synthesizes information, makes generalizations, builds arguments and applies problem-solving strategies

makes inferences and deductions and critiques solutions

verifies results of experiments

categorizes information appropriately

refines use of appropriate writing styles

evaluates different perspectives and formulates own opinion

applies ethical principles to the use of electronic note-taking

uses appropriate note-taking strategies, e.g., written bulleted points, computer-generated note-taking, clipboards, etc.

gathers specific additional information to support a hypothesis or problem-solving task

refines word processing, spreadsheet and database skills to organize information and create new ideas

consolidates use of computer-generated organizational strategies

Information Literacy Planning Organizer 7–12
Overview of Creating/Presenting Stage

Grade 7. Through planned learning activities the student:

understands the concept of "audience"

presents a solution to a problem using modeled examples which:

   debate an issue (argue for or against, or perhaps both)

   present ideas and information logically and are able to explain, profile, discuss and debate

   make simple generalizations and draw simple conclusions

creates written and oral reports, graphic, pictorial and dramatic presentations of similar complexity using modeled examples

creates presentations exhibiting synthesis of information

extends desktop publishing skills (graphics—borders, WordArt, clip art)

begins to construct multimedia presentations using modeled examples

uses e-mail to transfer and share information using modeled examples

is aware of Web page structure

Grade 8. Through planned learning activities the student:

understands the concept of "audience"

presents a solution to a problem through modeled examples which:

   debate an issue (argue for or against, or perhaps both)

   present ideas and information logically and are able to explain, profile, discuss and debate

   make simple generalizations and draw simple conclusions

creates written and oral reports, graphic, pictorial and dramatic presentations of similar complexity using modeled examples

consolidates desktop publishing skills (graphics—borders, WordArt, clip art)

constructs multimedia presentations using modeled examples

uses e-mail to transfer and share information through modeled examples

uses special software appropriate to the task through modeled examples

examines Web page construction

Grade 9. Through planned learning activities the student:

understands the concept of "audience"

presents a solution to a problem through modeled examples which:

   support an issue (argue for or against, or perhaps both)

   present ideas and information logically and are able to explain, profile, discuss and debate

   make simple generalizations and draw simple conclusions

   use some subject-specific words and phrases

creates written and oral reports, graphic, pictorial and dramatic presentations of similar complexity with guidance

consolidates desktop publishing skills (graphics—borders, WordArt, clip art)

constructs multimedia presentations with guidance

uses e-mail to transfer and share information with guidance

uses special software appropriate to the task with guidance

examines Web page construction

creates spreadsheets and databases using modeled examples

generates electronic charts, tables and graphs using modeled examples

presents information using a given format, e.g., oral reports and graphic, pictorial and dramatic presentation with guidance

Grade 10. Through planned learning activities the student:

understands the concept of "audience"

presents a solution to a problem or task with guidance which:

    supports an issue (argues for or against, or perhaps both)

    presents ideas and information logically and is able to explain, profile, discuss and debate

    makes simple generalizations and draws simple conclusions

    uses subject-specific words and phrases

creates written and oral reports, graphic, pictorial and dramatic presentations of similar complexity with guidance

refines desktop publishing skills (graphics—borders, WordArt, clip art)

constructs multimedia presentations with guidance

uses e-mail to transfer and share information

uses special software appropriate to the task with guidance

designs Web pages using modeled techniques

creates spreadsheets and databases with guidance

generates electronic charts, tables and graphs with guidance

presents information using a given format, e.g., oral reports and graphic, pictorial and dramatic presentations

Grade 11. Through planned learning activities the student:

creates an original response to a problem or task which:

    is analytical and persuasive, elaborating and justifying ideas where appropriate

    demonstrates objectivity and consideration of more than one viewpoint

    sustains subject-specific vocabulary throughout the task

creates written and oral reports, graphic, pictorial and dramatic presentations

refines desktop publishing skills

creates multimedia presentations

uses e-mail to transfer and share information

uses special software appropriate to the task

designs Web pages with guidance

creates original spreadsheets, databases

generates electronic charts, tables and graphs

presents information, selecting a form and organizing framework which demonstrate control over a variety of text structures

Grade 12. Through planned learning activities the student:

creates an original response to a problem or task which:

    is analytical and persuasive, elaborating and justifying ideas where appropriate

    demonstrates objectivity and consideration of more than one viewpoint

    sustains subject-specific vocabulary throughout the task

creates oral reports, graphic, pictorial and dramatic presentations

refines desktop publishing skills

creates multimedia presentations

uses e-mail to transfer and share information

uses special software appropriate to the task

designs Web pages

creates original spreadsheets, databases

generates electronic charts, tables and graphs

presents information, selecting a form and organizing framework which demonstrate control over a variety of text structures

Information Literacy Planning Organizer 7–12
Overview of Evaluating Stage

Grade 7. Through analysis of outcomes-based criteria the student:

respects the rights and opinions of others

considers the quantity, quality and relevance of information

assesses the student's own involvement with the topic or problem

reflects on and evaluates effectiveness of process used

evaluates personal ideas, feelings and actions and those of others

identifies questions and issues arising from decisions and actions

responds constructively to assessment by teachers

develops concept of peer evaluation by giving and receiving feedback

analyzes audience response to presentation using modeled examples

uses a variety of evaluative strategies using modeled examples to assess and review learning strengths and weaknesses, e.g.,
  reflective journals

evaluates understanding and implementation of the set task criteria using modeled examples

acknowledges personal and group achievements

Grade 8. Through analysis of outcomes-based criteria the student:

identifies skills using modeled techniques that require practice and refinement

responds constructively to assessment by teachers

accepts feedback from peers, caregivers, teachers and appropriate others

analyzes audience response to presentation using modeled examples

uses a variety of evaluative strategies using modeled examples to assess and review
  learning strengths and weaknesses, e.g., learning logs, reflective journals

evaluates understanding and implementation of the set task criteria using modeled examples

acknowledges personal and group achievements

Grade 9. Through analysis of outcomes-based criteria the student:

identifies skills with guidance that require practice and refinement

responds constructively to assessment by teachers

accepts feedback from peers, caregivers, teachers and appropriate others

analyzes audience response to presentation with guidance

uses a variety of evaluative strategies with guidance to assess and review learning strengths and weaknesses, e.g., learning logs,
  reflective journals

evaluates understanding and implementation of the set task criteria with guidance

acknowledges personal and group achievements

Grade 10. Through analysis of outcomes-based criteria the student:

identifies skills with guidance that require practice and refinement

responds to assessment by teachers

accepts feedback from peers, caregivers, teachers and appropriate others

analyzes audience response to presentation

uses a variety of evaluative strategies with guidance to assess and determine future learning pathways, e.g., learning logs,
  reflective journals

evaluates understanding and implementation of the set task criteria with guidance

acknowledges personal and group achievements

Information Literacy Planning Organizer 7–12
Overview of Evaluating Stage

Grade 11. Through analysis of outcomes-based criteria the student:

identifies skills that require practice and refinement and reflect on new learnings

responds to assessment by teachers

accepts feedback from peers, caregivers, teachers and appropriate others

analyzes audience response to presentation

uses a variety of evaluative strategies with guidance to assess and determine future learning pathways, e.g., learning logs, reflective journals

evaluates understanding and implementation of the set task criteria with guidance

acknowledges personal and group achievements

analyzes response to a problem accurately in terms of resources, constraints and objectives

analyzes the effectiveness of problem-solving strategies

Grade 12. Through analysis of outcomes-based criteria the student:

identifies skills that require practice and refinement and reflect on new learnings

responds to assessment by teachers

accepts feedback from peers, caregivers, teachers and appropriate others

analyzes audience response to presentation

uses a variety of evaluative strategies with guidance to assess and determine future learning pathways, e.g., learning logs, reflective journals

evaluates understanding and implementation of the set task criteria

acknowledges personal and group achievements

analyzes response to a problem accurately in terms of resources, constraints and objectives

analyzes the effectiveness of problem-solving strategies

Planning
Organizers

Part 1, "Process Overviews," provided a list of the stages and skills of the information literacy process across grade levels to show the sequential and developmental nature of the process. The planning organizers in part 2 pull together by grade level the list of skills given in the process overviews in part 1. In addition to the six stages of the information process (defining, locating, selecting/analyzing, organizing/ synthesizing, creating/presenting, and evaluating), grades K–2 planning organizers include orienting skills. These skills pertain to the general physical layout of the school and an awareness of significant school personnel. Other orienting skills refer to responsible behavior toward property and people.

At the beginning of each year, supply teachers with a copy of the planning organizer for their grade levels. They list the names of the units (or themes or topics) they will teach at the top of the first page of the planning organizer and in the vertical columns above the skills listings.

Next, working collaboratively, the teacher and the library media specialist decide which skills will be appropriate for each unit. They record their decisions by placing a check mark in the corresponding skill rows under that unit heading. Then they plan the learning activities, resources, and assessment tasks that relate to the selected skills for a unit. (Many activities to use when teaching selected skills in the information literacy program may be found in part 3 of this book.) The teacher and library media specialist also determine who will take responsibility for various activities, and they plan the instructional groups and spaces they will use. For example, a particular activity might be presented by the library media specialist to a small group in the library. Spaces or resources that require scheduling can be tentatively reserved at this time as well.

If collaborative planning and teaching of information literacy skills are not an option, the planning organizers may be used effectively by either teachers or library media specialists as a guide to the sequential development of skills and planned lessons. Teachers of students with special needs should have a full set of the K–6 planning organizers to facilitate their planning.

At the end of each school year, place the planning organizers in a central location as part of an ongoing validation process to ensure that there is a whole-school approach to information literacy. Encourage teachers to refer to them when planning for the following school year.

As an alternative to using the planning organizers, this activity could be completed by opening the two Excel files and copying the appropriate skills from the process overview file on the CD-ROM to create a planning organizer by grade level. Then the specific skills for each unit could be copied to a second file and printed and stored as a record for the unit.

Grade 7 Planning Organizer

Class Teacher/s: **Class:**   **Year:**

Unit: _____ Date:

Unit: _____ Date:

Unit: _____ Date:

Unit: _____ Date:

Unit: _____ Date:

Unit: _____ Date:

Unit: _____ Date:

Unit: _____ Date:

Units

INFORMATION PROCESS

DEFINING. Through planned learning activities the student:

INFORMATION PROCESS								
develops appropriate questioning techniques through extensive modeling to clarify requirements of task								
selects from a range of topics using modeled techniques								
draws on prior knowledge to brainstorm and cluster ideas								
identifies and interprets key words in task using modeled techniques								
develops focus questions using modeled techniques								
devises a time-management strategy to meet given deadlines using modeled techniques								
selects an appropriate strategy using modeled examples to record headings and subheadings								
makes predictions using models provided about likely sources of information onto search strategy sheet								
clarifies and refines research questions using modeled techniques								
re-defines problem with guidance when alternative solutions are exhausted								
formulates a basic hypothesis using modeled techniques								

Grade 7 Planning Organizer

LOCATING. Through planned learning activities the student:

- follows a search plan using key words and related terms, modifying where necessary
- determines the type of resource most appropriate for the topic
- identifies and locates print and non-print resources including:
  - understanding organization of resources in school and local libraries
  - recognizing the value of fiction for specific topics, e.g., historical fiction
  - becoming familiar with limited number of appropriate search engines using modeled techniques
  - using simple and combined terms to search catalog, Net and CD-ROM sources
  - choosing broader or narrower terms to refine search results
  - using Help function to locate information and refine searches
  - searching for information using given Internet addresses and managing bookmarks
  - using information from the wider community
- identifies appropriate resources by:
  - using skimming and scanning techniques to survey readability in electronic and print resources
  - using contents, index and text headings for all types of resources including electronic
- recognizes where currency of information is necessary
- recognizes the need to locate a variety of resources representing a range of views
- with guidance, extends use of Internet/e-mail by:
  - using given Internet addresses with assistance
  - bookmarking a location
  - composing and sending e-mail
  - accessing and reading e-mail
  - replying to an e-mail message
  - forwarding an e-mail message
  - copying/pasting from Web page to document
  - being aware of Internet search engines as a source of information
  - being aware of Web page structure
- extends use of computer system skills using modeled examples by:
  - deleting, copying and moving files
  - loading software for information retrieval
- selectively printing information from electronic sources under teacher supervision

Grade 7 Planning Organizer

LOCATING [cont]. Through planned learning activities the student:

- identifies and locates information from both primary and secondary sources using modeled techniques
- uses special print and non-print reference resources using modeled examples
- recognizes difference in purpose of magazines, newspapers, pamphlets using modeled techniques
- uses range of equipment to access information, e.g., telephone, fax, computer, scanner, digital camera using modeled techniques
- uses e-mail to discuss topics and to facilitate cooperative activities using modeled examples

SELECTING/ANALYZING. Through planned learning activities the student:

- selects resources using modeled techniques by:
  - skimming and scanning
  - using contents, index and text headings
- evaluates appropriateness of resources, discarding if necessary
- modifies focus questions using modeled techniques
- devises appropriate note-taking templates using modeled examples
- records information using modeled examples by:
  - using a note-making strategy appropriate to source and problem, e.g., concept mapping, outline
  - clustering electronic notes under subheadings
  - using a clipboard
  - selecting appropriate graphic organizer
- makes comparisons between the purpose of different writing styles using modeled examples, e.g., Information Report, Persuasive Essay, etc.
- compares information from different sources for opposing viewpoints and accuracy using modeled techniques
- recognizes the need for adequate data before drawing conclusions
- downloads text files from Internet sites using modeled techniques
- records bibliographic sources of information using author, title, publisher, date, http, date of download using modeled examples
- understands and complies with copyright requirements using modeled examples
- observes netiquette conventions when communicating electronically using modeled techniques
- understands there may be various interpretations of data
- uses a variety of primary and secondary sources using modeled examples

Grade 7 Planning Organizer

ORGANIZING/SYNTHESIZING. Through planned learning activities the student:

synthesizes selected information connecting similar ideas and begins to predict possible outcomes								
engages in reflective thinking to analyze and clarify a problem								
engages in group discussion to analyze and clarify a problem								
is aware there may be alternative solutions to a problem								
proposes a solution to a set problem based on prior knowledge and new information which:								
organize ideas and information logically								
make simple generalizations and draw simple conclusions								
verifies results of experiments using modeled examples								
categorizes information according to a framework of headings and subheadings using modeled examples								
consolidates the use of word processing skills by:								
selectively cutting and pasting information from an electronic source with guidance								
making notes using word processor or other software to quote a source or make notes								
making notes directly from screen								
using keyboard drills, Spelling, Grammar Check, Undo, Select all, Page Setup								
using lists/bullets								
creating and inserting simple tables								
wrapping text around graphics								
formatting text appropriate to text type								
creates computer-generated organizational strategies, e.g., flow charts, time lines using modeled examples								
makes notes using modeled techniques, e.g., written bulleted points, note-taking template, clipboards, etc.								
extends the use of databases with guidance by:								
browsing, editing and adding records in a class-created database								
sorting and deleting records								
using Find function to search for specific criteria								
consolidates the use of spreadsheets by:								
changing column width, row height and alignment								
using simple formulas for basic operations--multiply, subtract and divide								
develops the ability to have faith in own judgment and point of view								
recognizes information deficiencies and locates additional information								

Grade 7 Planning Organizer

CREATING/PRESENTING. Through planned learning activities the student:

- understands the concept of "audience"
- presents a solution to a problem using modeled examples which:
  - debate an issue (argue for or against, or perhaps both)
  - present ideas and information logically and are able to explain, profile, discuss and debate
  - make simple generalizations and draw simple conclusions
- creates written and oral reports, graphic, pictorial and dramatic presentations of similar complexity using modeled examples
- creates presentations exhibiting synthesis of information
- extends desktop publishing skills (graphics--borders, WordArt, clip art)
- begins to construct multimedia presentations using modeled examples
- uses e-mail to transfer and share information using modeled examples
- is aware of Web page structure

EVALUATING. Through analysis of outcomes-based criteria the student:

- respects the rights and opinions of others
- considers the quantity, quality and relevance of information
- assesses the student's own involvement with the topic or problem
- reflects on and evaluates effectiveness of process used
- evaluates personal ideas, feelings and actions and those of others
- identifies questions and issues arising from decisions and actions
- responds constructively to assessment by teachers
- develops concept of peer evaluation by giving and receiving feedback
- analyzes audience response to presentation using modeled examples
- uses a variety of evaluative strategies using modeled examples to assess and review learning strengths and weaknesses,
  - e.g., learning logs, reflective journals
- evaluates understanding and implementation of the set task criteria using modeled examples
- acknowledges personal and group achievements

Grade 8 Planning Organizer

Subject Teacher: **Class group/s:** **Year:**

Subject: **Units**

INFORMATION PROCESS

DEFINING. Through planned learning activities the student:

- develops appropriate questioning techniques through extensive modeling to clarify requirements of task
- **analyzes and clarifies a given task using modeled techniques**
- selects from a range of topics using modeled techniques
- **draws on prior knowledge to brainstorm and cluster ideas with teachers and peers**
- identifies and interprets key words in task using modeled techniques
- develops focus questions using modeled techniques
- devises a time-management strategy to meet given deadlines using modeled techniques
- selects an appropriate strategy using modeled examples to record headings and subheadings
- makes predictions using models provided about likely sources of information onto search strategy sheet
- clarifies and refines research questions using modeled techniques
- re-defines problem with guidance when alternative solutions are exhausted
- formulates a basic hypothesis using modeled techniques

LOCATING. Through planned learning activities the student:

- identifies and locates text and nontext resources including:
- understanding organization of resources in school and local libraries
- recognizing the value of fiction for specific topics, e.g., historical fiction
- using information from the wider community
- **accessing periodical indexes using modeled techniques**
- extends use of Internet/e-mail with guidance by:
- **becoming familiar with limited number of appropriate search engines using modeled techniques**
- composing and sending e-mail
- accessing and reading e-mail
- replying to and forwarding an e-mail message
- using e-mail to discuss topics and to facilitate cooperative activities using modeled examples
- **searching for information using given URLs and managing bookmarks**
- copying/pasting from Web page to document
- **extends the use of databases with guidance by:**
- using simple and Boolean terms to search catalog, Net and CD-ROM sources
- choosing broader or narrower terms to refine search results
- using Help function to locate information and refine searches

Grade 8 Planning Organizer

LOCATING [cont]. Through planned learning activities the student:

recognizes where currency of information is necessary				
recognizes the need to locate a variety of resources representing a range of views				
identifies and locates information from both primary and secondary sources using modeled techniques				
uses special print and non-print reference resources using modeled examples				
recognizes difference in purpose of magazines, newspapers, pamphlets using modeled techniques				
uses range of equipment to access information, e.g., telephone, fax, computer, scanner, digital camera using modeled techniques				
extends use of computer systems skills using modeled examples by:				
deleting, copying and moving files				
loading software for information retrieval				
selectively printing information from electronic sources				

SELECTING/ANALYZING. Through planned learning activities the student:

selects resources using modeled techniques by:				
skimming and scanning				
using contents, index and text headings				
evaluates appropriateness of resources, discarding if necessary				
modifies focus questions using modeled techniques				
devises appropriate note-taking templates using modeled examples				
records information using modeled examples by:				
using a note-making strategy appropriate to source and problem, e.g., concept mapping, outline				
recognizing when a note-making format requires modification				
clustering electronic notes under subheadings				
selecting appropriate graphic organizer				
makes comparisons between different text types using modeled examples, e.g., Information Report, Persuasive Essay, etc.				
compares information from different sources for opposing viewpoints and accuracy using modeled techniques				
records bibliographic sources of information using author, title, publisher, date, http, date of download using modeled examples				
understands and complies with copyright requirements using modeled examples				
downloads text files from Internet sites using modeled techniques				
observes netiquette conventions when communicating electronically using modeled techniques				
understands there may be various interpretations of data				
uses a variety of primary and secondary sources using modeled examples				

Grade 8 Planning Organizer

ORGANIZING/SYNTHESIZING. Through planned learning activities the student:

synthesizes information from a variety of sources using modeled examples

combines selected information connecting similar ideas and begins to predict possible outcomes

is aware of alternative consequences of solutions to a problem

proposes a solution to a set problem based on prior knowledge and new information which:

organize ideas and information logically

make simple generalizations and draw simple conclusions

verifies results of experiments through modeled examples

categorizes information according to a framework of headings and subheadings using modeled examples

consolidates the use of word processing skills by:

selectively cutting and pasting information from an electronic source with guidance

making notes using word processor or other software to quote a source or make notes

making notes directly from screen

using keyboard drills, Spelling, Grammar Check, Undo, Select all, Page Setup

using lists/bullets

creating and inserting simple tables

wrapping text around graphics

formatting text appropriate to writing styles

creates computer-generated organizational strategies, e.g., flow charts, time lines using modeled examples

makes notes using modeled techniques, e.g., written bulleted points, note-taking template, clipboards, etc.

extends the use of databases with guidance by:

browsing, editing and adding records in a class-created database

sorting and deleting records

using Find function to search for specific criteria

consolidates the use of spreadsheets by:

changing column width, row height and alignment

using simple formulas for basic operations--add, multiply, subtract and divide

develops the ability to have faith in own judgment and point of view

recognizes information deficiencies and locates additional information

Grade 8 Planning Organizer

CREATING/PRESENTING. Through planned learning activities the student:

understands the concept of "audience"

presents a solution to a problem through modeled examples which:

debate an issue (argue for or against, or perhaps both)

present ideas and information logically and are able to explain, profile, discuss and debate

make simple generalizations and draw simple conclusions

creates written and oral reports, graphic, pictorial and dramatic presentations of similar complexity using modeled examples

consolidates desktop publishing skills (graphics--borders, WordArt, clip art)

constructs multimedia presentations through modeled examples

uses e-mail to transfer and share information through modeled examples

uses special software appropriate to the task through modeled examples

examines Web page construction

EVALUATING. Through analysis of outcomes-based criteria the student:

identifies skills using modeled techniques that require practice and refinement

responds constructively to assessment by teachers

accepts feedback from peers, caregivers, teachers and appropriate others

analyzes audience response to presentation using modeled examples

uses a variety of evaluative strategies using modeled examples to assess and review learning strengths and weaknesses,

e.g., learning logs, reflective journals

evaluates understanding and implementation of the set task criteria using modeled examples

acknowledges personal and group achievements

Grade 9 Planning Organizer

Subject Teacher:		Year:					
Subject:	Class group/s:			Units			

INFORMATION PROCESS

DEFINING. Through planned learning activities the student:

consolidates appropriate questioning techniques with guidance to clarify requirements of task

selects from a range of topics with guidance

draws on prior knowledge to brainstorm and cluster ideas

identifies and interprets key words in task with guidance

develops focus questions with guidance

devises a time-management strategy with guidance to meet given deadlines

selects an appropriate strategy with guidance to record headings and subheadings

makes predictions with guidance about likely sources of information onto search strategy sheet

clarifies and refines research questions with guidance

uses reference sources to clarify the meaning of a research task

re-defines problem with guidance when alternative solutions are exhausted

formulates a basic hypothesis with guidance

LOCATING. Through planned learning activities the student:

identifies and locates text and nontext resources including:

understanding organization of resources in school and local libraries

recognizing the value of fiction for specific topics, e.g., historical fiction

accessing periodical indexes with guidance

extends the use of Internet/e-mail by:

becoming familiar with limited number of appropriate search engines with guidance

using e-mail with guidance to discuss topics and to facilitate cooperative activities

using e-mail to access experts in the field

searching for information using given URLs and managing bookmarks

extends the use of databases with guidance by:

using simple and Boolean terms to search catalog, Net and CD-ROM sources

choosing broader or narrower terms to refine search results

using Help function to locate information and refine searches

extends use of computer systems skills with guidance by:

deleting, copying and moving files

selectively printing information from electronic sources

accesses community and government information sources

Grade 9 Planning Organizer

LOCATING [cont]. Through planned learning activities the student:

recognizes where currency of information is necessary

recognizes the need to locate a variety of resources representing a range of views

identifies and locates information from both primary and secondary sources with guidance

uses special print and non-print reference resources with guidance

recognizes difference in purpose of magazines, newspapers, pamphlets with guidance

uses range of equipment to access information, e.g., telephone, fax, computer, scanner, digital camera

SELECTING/ANALYZING. Through planned learning activities the student:

selects resources with guidance by:

skimming and scanning

using contents, index and text headings

analyzes appropriate information using modeled techniques from a variety of sources, including exhibitions, excursions,

audio and visual recordings and interviews by:

using text/context clues such as text headings and subheadings

identifying main and subordinate ideas

re-reading, re-listening and re-viewing

evaluates appropriateness of resources, discarding if necessary

modifies focus questions with guidance

devises appropriate note-taking templates with guidance

records information with guidance by:

devising note-making strategies to ensure information is collected consistently and accurately

modifying note-making formats as appropriate to the task and information source

clustering notes under subheadings

selecting appropriate graphic organizer

makes comparisons with guidance between different text types, e.g., Information Report, Persuasive Essay, etc.

compares information from different sources for opposing viewpoints and accuracy with guidance

records bibliographic sources of information using author, title, publisher, date, http, date of download with guidance

understands and complies with copyright requirements with guidance

downloads text and graphic files from Internet sites with guidance

observes netiquette conventions with guidance

considers a range of viewpoints by:

recognizing when the information is fact or opinion

identifying authority, purpose and intended audience of source

identifying bias and omission in information sources

uses a variety of primary and secondary sources with guidance

understands strategies may be to used to slant information in subtle ways using modeled techniques

using prior knowledge, proposes problem-solving strategies for real-life situations

Grade 9 Planning Organizer

ORGANIZING/SYNTHESIZING. Through planned learning activities the student:

combines selected information connecting similar ideas

draws inferences from evidence with guidance

synthesizes information to predict consequences and to construct generalizations with guidance

proposes a solution to a set problem based on prior knowledge and new information which:

organize ideas and information logically

make simple generalizations and draw simple conclusions

verifies results of experiments with guidance

categorizes information according to a framework of headings, subheadings or database fields with guidance

consolidates the use of word processing skills by:

selectively cutting and pasting information from an electronic source with guidance

making notes using word processor or other software to quote a source or make notes

making notes directly from screen

using Spelling, Grammar Check, Undo, Select all, Page Setup

using lists/bullets

creating and inserting simple tables

wrapping text around graphics

formatting text appropriate to writing styles

creates computer-generated organizational strategies with guidance, e.g., flow charts, time lines

makes notes with guidance, e.g., written bulleted points, note-taking template, clipboards, etc.

extends the use of databases with guidance by:

browsing, editing and adding records in a database

sorting and deleting records

using Find function to search for specific criteria

consolidates the use of spreadsheets by:

changing column width, row height and alignment

using simple formulas for basic operations--add, multiply, subtract and divide

responds appropriately to the given writing styles, e.g., argument, report, etc.

identifies positive and negative influences in information sources with guidance

recognizes information deficiencies and locates additional information

Grade 9 Planning Organizer

CREATING/PRESENTING. Through planned learning activities the student:

understands the concept of "audience"

presents a solution to a problem through modeled examples which:

    support an issue (argue for or against, or perhaps both)

    present ideas and information logically and are able to explain, profile, discuss and debate

    make simple generalizations and draw simple conclusions

    use some subject-specific words and phrases

creates written and oral reports, graphic, pictorial and dramatic presentations of similar complexity with guidance

consolidates desktop publishing skills (graphics--borders, WordArt, clip art)

constructs multimedia presentations with guidance

uses e-mail to transfer and share information with guidance

uses special software appropriate to the task with guidance

examines Web page construction

creates spreadsheets and databases using modeled examples

generates electronic charts, tables and graphs using modeled examples

presents information using a given format, e.g., oral reports and graphic, pictorial and dramatic presentation with guidance

EVALUATING. Through analysis of outcomes-based criteria the student:

identifies skills with guidance that require practice and refinement

responds constructively to assessment by teachers

accepts feedback from peers, caregivers, teachers and appropriate others

analyzes audience response to presentation with guidance

uses a variety of evaluative strategies with guidance to assess and review learning strengths and weaknesses, e.g., learning logs, reflective journals

evaluates understanding and implementation of the set task criteria with guidance

acknowledges personal and group achievements

Grade 10 Planning Organizer

Subject Teacher:	Year:
Subject:	Class group/s:	Units

INFORMATION PROCESS

DEFINING. Through planned learning activities the student:

- **refines appropriate questioning techniques with guidance to clarify requirements of task**
- **selects from a range of topics**
- draws on prior knowledge to brainstorm and cluster ideas
- **identifies and interprets key words in task**
- develops focus questions with guidance
- **devises a time-management strategy to meet given deadlines**
- **selects an appropriate strategy to record headings and subheadings**
- makes predictions with guidance about likely sources of information onto search strategy sheet
- clarifies and refines research questions with guidance
- uses reference sources to clarify the meaning of a research task
- re-defines problem with assistance when alternative solutions are exhausted
- **negotiates and justifies alternative tasks as appropriate**
- formulates a hypothesis with guidance

LOCATING. Through planned learning activities the student:

- identifies and locates text and nontext resources including:
- **understanding organization of resources in school, local and state libraries**
- recognizing the significance of cross-references and subtopics in an index
- extends the use of Internet/e-mail by:
- **becoming familiar with a variety of appropriate search engines**
- using e-mail to discuss topics and to facilitate cooperative activities
- using e-mail to access experts in the field
- searching for information using given URLs and managing bookmarks
- **views, downloads and decompresses files from Internet sites with guidance**
- **observes netiquette conventions**
- **extends the use of databases by:**
- using simple and Boolean terms to search catalog, Net and CD-ROM sources
- choosing broader or narrower terms to refine search results
- using Help function to locate information and refine searches
- **uses electronic indexes using modeled examples to locate current information**
- **extends the use of computer systems skills by:**
- deleting, copying and moving files
- selectively printing information from electronic sources

Grade 10 Planning Organizer

LOCATING [cont]. Through planned learning activities the student:

accesses community and government information sources

recognizes where currency of information is necessary

recognizes the need to locate a variety of resources representing a range of views

identifies and locates information from both primary and secondary sources

recognizes difference in purpose of magazines, newspapers, pamphlets

uses special print and non-print reference resources

recognizes the "positioning" of the reader by the author

uses range of equipment to access information, e.g., telephone, fax, computer, scanner, digital camera

SELECTING/ANALYZING. Through planned learning activities the student:

analyzes appropriate information from a variety of sources, including exhibitions, excursions, audio and visual recordings and interviews by:

using text/context clues such as text headings and subheadings

identifying main and subordinate ideas

re-reading, re-listening and re-viewing

evaluates appropriateness of resources, discarding if necessary

modifies focus questions

devises appropriate note-taking templates

records information by:

devising note-making strategies to ensure information is collected consistently and accurately

modifying note-making formats as appropriate to the task and information source

clustering notes under subheadings

selecting appropriate graphic organizer

makes comparisons between different text types, e.g., Information Report, Persuasive Essay, etc.

compares information from different sources for opposing viewpoints and accuracy

analyzes information deficiencies and locates additional information

records bibliographic sources of information using author, title, publisher, date, http, date of download

understands and complies with copyright requirements

views, downloads and decompresses files from Internet sites with guidance

observes netiquette conventions

considers a range of viewpoints by:

recognizing when the information is fact or opinion

identifying authority, purpose and intended audience of resource

analyzes statistical data using modeled techniques

uses a variety of primary and secondary sources

identifies strategies used to slant information in subtle ways

using prior knowledge and new learnings, proposes problem-solving strategies for real-life situations

Grade 10 Planning Organizer

ORGANIZING/SYNTHESIZING. Through planned learning activities the student:

combines selected information connecting similar ideas

draws inferences from evidence

synthesizes information to predict consequences and to construct generalizations with guidance

proposes a solution to a set problem based on prior knowledge and new information which:

organize ideas and information logically

make generalizations and draw conclusions

verifies results of experiments with guidance

categorizes information according to a framework of headings, subheadings or database fields

consolidates the use of word processing skills by:

creating computer-generated organizational strategies with guidance, e.g., flow charts, time lines

making notes, e.g., written bulleted points, note-taking template, clipboards, etc.

extends the use of databases with guidance by:

browsing, editing and adding records in a database

sorting and deleting records

using Find function to search for specific criteria

consolidates the use of spreadsheets by:

changing column width, row height and alignment

using simple formulas for basic operations--add, multiply, subtract and divide

responds appropriately to the given text type, e.g., Information Report, Persuasive Essay

identifies positive and negative influences in information sources

recognizes information deficiencies and locates additional information

Grade 10 Planning Organizer

CREATING/PRESENTING. Through planned learning activities the student:

understands the concept of "audience"

presents a solution to a problem or task with guidance which:

supports an issue (argues for or against, or perhaps both)

presents ideas and information logically and is able to explain, profile, discuss and debate

makes simple generalizations and draws simple conclusions

uses subject-specific words and phrases

creates written and oral reports, graphic, pictorial and dramatic presentations of similar complexity with guidance

refines desktop publishing skills (graphics--borders, WordArt, clip art)

constructs multimedia presentations with guidance

uses e-mail to transfer and share information

uses special software appropriate to the task with guidance

designs Web pages using modeled techniques

creates spreadsheets and databases with guidance

generates electronic charts, tables and graphs with guidance

presents information using a given format, e.g., oral reports and graphic, pictorial and dramatic presentations

EVALUATING. Through analysis of outcomes-based criteria, the student:

identifies skills with guidance that require practice and refinement

responds to assessment by teachers

accepts feedback from peers, caregivers, teachers and appropriate others

analyzes audience response to presentation

uses a variety of evaluative strategies with guidance to assess and determine future learning pathways, e.g., learning logs, reflective journals

evaluates understanding and implementation of the set task criteria with guidance

acknowledges personal and group achievements

Grade 11 Planning Organizer

Subject Teacher:

Year:

Subject:

Class group/s:

Unit

INFORMATION PROCESS

DEFINING. Through planned learning activities the student:

refines appropriate questioning techniques to clarify requirements of task

selects from a range of topics

draws on prior knowledge to brainstorm and cluster ideas

identifies and interprets key words in task

develops questions and responds to a task with guidance which may require:

identification of trends, analysis, critical evaluation, survey, cause and effect

devises a time-management strategy to meet given deadlines

selects an appropriate strategy to record headings and subheadings

makes predictions about likely sources of information onto search strategy sheet

clarifies and refines research questions

uses reference sources to explore a topic and identify issues and subtopics with guidance

re-defines problem when alternative solutions are exhausted

negotiates and justifies alternative tasks as appropriate

formulates a hypothesis

LOCATING. Through planned learning activities the student:

accesses all types of text and information technologies, including:

understanding organization of resources in school, local and state libraries

surveying all aspects of a resource and recognizing the significance of cross-references and subtopics

searching appropriate databases within the school and wider community

using advanced search techniques to refine search results

using e-mail to access experts in the field

uses e-mail to discuss topics and to facilitate cooperative activities

selectively prints information from electronic sources

uses electronic indexes with guidance to locate current information

accesses community and government information sources

recognizes where currency of information is necessary

recognizes the need to locate a variety of resources representing a range of views

identifies and locates information from both primary and secondary sources

recognizes difference in purpose of magazines, newspapers, pamphlets

uses knowledge of coverage and purpose of resources to refine the scope of the search

Grade 11 Planning Organizer

LOCATING [cont]. Through planned learning activities the student:

recognizes the "positioning" of the reader by the author

uses special print and non-print reference resources

uses range of equipment to access information, e.g., telephone, fax, computer, scanner, digital camera

SELECTING/ANALYZING. Through planned learning activities the student:

interprets, compares and selects information with guidance after:

evaluating information for accuracy, bias and omission

evaluating an argument for logic

examining reasons for value judgments

examining reasons for contradictions or seeming contradictions in evidence

devises appropriate note-taking templates

records information by:

devising note-making strategies to ensure information is collected consistently and accurately

modifying note-making formats as appropriate to the task and information source

understands and complies with copyright requirements

views, downloads and decompresses files from Internet sites

observes netiquette conventions

analyzes statistical data with guidance

uses a variety of primary and secondary sources

using prior knowledge, proposes problem-solving strategies for real-life situations

records bibliographic source using a recognized system of notation

ORGANIZING/SYNTHESIZING. Through planned learning activities the student:

tests hypotheses statistically using modeled examples

combines selected information connecting similar ideas

synthesizes information, makes generalizations, builds arguments and applies problem-solving strategies

makes inferences and deductions and critiques solutions

verifies results of experiments

categorizes information according to a framework of headings, subheadings or database fields

refines use of appropriate writing styles

evaluates different perspectives and formulates own opinion

applies ethical principles to the use of electronic note-taking

uses appropriate note-taking strategies, e.g., written bulleted points, computer-generated note-taking, clipboards, etc.

Grade 11 Planning Organizer

ORGANIZING/SYNTHESIZING [cont]. Through planned learning activities the student:

gathers specific additional information to support a hypothesis or problem-solving task

refines word processing, spreadsheet and database skills to organize information and create new ideas

consolidates use of computer-generated organizational strategies

CREATING/PRESENTING. Through planned learning activities the student:

creates an original response to a problem or task which:

is analytical and persuasive, elaborating and justifying ideas where appropriate

demonstrates objectivity and consideration of more than one viewpoint

sustains subject-specific vocabulary throughout the task

creates written and oral reports, graphic, pictorial and dramatic presentations

refines desktop publishing skills

creates multimedia presentations

uses e-mail to transfer and share information

uses special software appropriate to the task

designs Web pages with guidance

creates original spreadsheets, databases

generates electronic charts, tables and graphs

presents information, selecting a form and organizing framework which demonstrates control over a variety of text structures

EVALUATING. Through analysis of outcomes-based criteria the student:

identifies skills that require practice and refinement and reflect on new learnings

responds to assessment by teachers

accepts feedback from peers, caregivers, teachers and appropriate others

analyzes audience response to presentation

uses a variety of evaluative strategies with guidance to assess and determine future learning pathways, e.g., learning logs, reflective journals

evaluates understanding and implementation of the set task criteria with guidance

acknowledges personal and group achievements

analyzes response to a problem accurately in terms of resources, constraints and objectives

analyzes the effectiveness of problem-solving strategies

Grade 12 Planning Organizer

Subject Teacher:	Year:											
Subject:						Units						
Class group/s:												

DEFINING. Through planned learning activities the student:

refines appropriate questioning techniques to clarify requirements of task

selects from a range of topics

draws on prior knowledge to brainstorm and cluster ideas

identifies and interprets key words in task

develops focus questions and responds to a task which may require identification of trends, analysis, critical evaluation, survey, cause and effect

devises a time-management strategy to meet given deadlines

selects an appropriate strategy to record heading and subheadings

makes predictions about likely sources of information onto search strategy sheet

clarifies and refines research questions

uses reference sources to explore a topic and identify issues and subtopics

re-defines problem when alternative solutions are exhausted

negotiates and justifies alternative tasks as appropriate

formulates a hypothesis

LOCATING. Through planned learning activities the student:

accesses all types of text and information technologies, including:

understanding organization of resources in school, local and state libraries

surveying all aspects of a resource and recognizing the significance of cross-references and subtopics

searching appropriate databases within the school and wider community

using advanced search techniques to refine search results

using e-mail to access experts in the field

uses e-mail to discuss topics and to facilitate cooperative activities

selectively prints information from electronic sources

uses electronic indexes to locate current information

accesses community and government information sources

recognizes where currency of information is necessary

recognizes when resources represent different perspectives

identifies and locates information from both primary and secondary sources

recognizes difference in purpose of magazines, newspapers, pamphlets

recognizes the "positioning" of the reader by the author

uses special print and non-print reference resources

uses range of equipment to access information, e.g., telephone, fax, computer, scanner, digital camera

Grade 12 Planning Organizer

SELECTING/ANALYZING. Through planned learning activities the student:

interprets, compares and selects information after:

evaluating information for accuracy, bias and omission											
evaluating an argument for logic											
examining reasons for value judgments											
examining reasons for contradictions or seeming contradictions in evidence											
devises appropriate note-taking templates											
records information by:											
devising note-making strategies to ensure information is collected consistently and accurately											
modifying note-making formats as appropriate to the task and information source											
understands and complies with copyright requirements											
views, downloads and decompresses files from Internet sites											
observes netiquette conventions											
analyzes statistical data											
uses a variety of primary and secondary sources											
using prior knowledge, proposes problem-solving strategies for real-life situations											
records bibliographic source											
correctly cites footnotes and endnotes											

ORGANIZING/SYNTHESIZING. Through planned learning activities the student:

tests hypotheses statistically											
combines selected information connecting similar ideas											
synthesizes information, makes generalizations, builds arguments and applies problem-solving strategies											
makes inferences and deductions and critiques solutions											
verifies results of experiments											
categorizes information appropriately											
refines use of appropriate writing styles											
evaluates different perspectives and formulates own opinion											
applies ethical principles to the use of electronic note-taking											
uses appropriate note-taking strategies, e.g., written bulleted points, computer-generated note-taking, clipboards, etc.											
gathers specific additional information to support a hypothesis or problem-solving task											
refines word processing, spreadsheet and database skills to organize information and create new ideas											
consolidates use of computer-generated organizational strategies											

Grade 12 Planning Organizer

CREATING/PRESENTING. Through planned learning activities the student:

creates an original response to a problem or task which:

is analytical and persuasive, elaborating and justifying ideas where appropriate

demonstrates objectivity and consideration of more than one viewpoint

sustains subject-specific vocabulary throughout the task

creates oral reports, graphic, pictorial and dramatic presentations

refines desktop publishing skills

creates multimedia presentations

uses e-mail to transfer and share information

uses special software appropriate to the task

designs Web pages

creates original spreadsheets, databases

generates electronic charts, tables and graphs

presents information, selecting a form and organizing framework which demonstrates control

over a variety of text structures

EVALUATING. Through analysis of outcomes-based criteria the student:

identifies skills that require practice and refinement and reflect on new learnings

responds to assessment by teachers

accepts feedback from peers, caregivers, teachers and appropriate others

analyzes audience response to presentation

uses a variety of evaluative strategies with guidance to assess and determine future learning pathways, e.g., learning logs, reflective journals

evaluates understanding and implementation of the set task criteria

acknowledges personal and group achievements

analyzes response to a problem accurately in terms of resources, constraints and objectives

analyzes the effectiveness of problem-solving strategies

3

Teaching Tools

The teaching tools are reproducible forms that support the teaching of information literacy skills across the curriculum. These teaching support worksheets and strategies complement the information literacy planning organizers developed in part 2.

The worksheets are designed to

- provide a comprehensive structure for teaching information literacy using the six-stage information literacy process—defining, locating, selecting/analyzing, organizing/synthesizing, creating/presenting, and evaluating

- provide a generic framework for use across the curriculum

- encourage students to develop a consistent approach to research tasks

- assist teachers with the teaching of information literacy skills (teaching tips for selected skills are included to stimulate teaching ideas)

- assist a wide range of teaching professionals including teachers of ESL, students with special needs, etc.

How to Use the Teaching Tools

As explained in part 2, teachers and library media specialists collaboratively plan units using the school-based information literacy planning organizers. After the relevant skills have been identified for inclusion in the unit, the planners decide on activities to develop these skills. Teachers and the library media specialist select from the teaching tools those activities that support the instruction of these skills according to the curriculum content of the unit and appropriate assessment tasks. The teaching tools contain activities based on a broad range of developmental levels and student competencies.

Student Competencies

To be prepared for the twenty-first century, students must have the competencies and skills to learn and think creatively, make informed decisions, and solve problems. They need to organize information and process symbols, acquire and apply new knowledge and skills, and make connections to relationships when solving a problem. The information literacy skills as set out in the planning organizers will assist students in acquiring these skills and in developing personal qualities. The personal qualities include those identified by the U.S. Secretary of Labor's Commission on Achieving Necessary Skills:

- *Responsibility*—exerts a high level of effort and perseveres toward goal attainment

- *Self-esteem*—believes in own self-worth and maintains a positive view of self

- *Sociability*—demonstrates understanding, friendliness, adaptability, empathy, and politeness in group settings

- *Self-management*—assesses self accurately, sets personal goals, monitors progress, and exhibits self-control

- *Integrity/honesty*—chooses ethical courses of action[1]

During the course of our daily lives we are constantly problem solving—making choices based on prior knowledge combined with new information to create new knowledge. To develop skills in problem solving and to overcome the problem of plagiarism, students must be given the opportunity to offer original solutions to a problem. Therefore, teachers are encouraged to frame a unit of work as a problem or task rather than as a topic so that students will create and present original ideas instead of simply reading and regurgitating the knowledge of others. Students are challenged and are frequently far more motivated by the prospect of solving a problem, particularly if the problem can be related to their own experiences or real-life situations. Many teachers have indicated that students often achieve outcomes far beyond expectations when offered a problem-solving task.

The following examples highlight the difference between defining a unit as a topic versus as a problem to be solved or a task to be accomplished:

Topic: Celebrations

Problem/Task: What do we need to do to prepare a birthday party for someone?

Topic: Native Animals

Problem/Task: If you were designing a zoo for native animals, which animals would you choose to show visitors to your country? Design an animal enclosure for one of these animals to show how it lives in its natural environment.

Problems or tasks call for active participation of students. When defining units in terms of a problem or task, teachers and library media specialists will want to use specific verbs, such as the following:

advertise	classify	construct	discuss
improve	devise	create	invent
investigate	use	predict	plan
build	identify	explain	separate
solve	show	illustrate	select
choose	decide	design	imagine
prepare			

Embedding Technology in the Information Process

The table on pages 48–49 is an example of how technology may be embedded in the information process. It includes a comparison between print-based or low-tech and high-tech approaches to problem solving or task completion. The high-tech examples use currently available software.

Using the Unit Planner

The unit planner (see page 47) pulls together plans for all aspects of a unit. Teachers and library media specialists can work together to complete a unit planner for each unit they include in their planning organizers (see part 2). They may start by defining the purpose of the unit as a problem or task and recording it at the top of the form. Then they can transfer the list of skills for that unit from their overall planning sheets created in part 2. Next, they can determine the activities that are appropriate for those skills, pulling from the teaching tools blackline masters and from activities of their own creation. They determine how they will assess whether students have mastered those skills or shown an adequate grasp of the process and record those criteria in the assessment column. Finally, using the embedding technology chart supplemented by their own knowledge of locally available resources, they record the high-tech or low-tech resources they plan to have students use in each stage of the information literacy process for solving the unit's problem or completing its task. By using this planning sheet, teachers and library media specialists have a complete overview of a unit that includes all aspects of the information literacy process.

NOTE

1. U.S. Dept. of Labor, Secretary's Commission on Achieving Necessary Skills (SCANS), *What Work Requires of Schools: A SCANS Report for America 2000* (Washington, D.C.: U.S. Dept. of Labor, 1991), xvii–xviii.

Unit Planner

Class teacher/s:	Class/group:	Commencing date:	Duration of unit:	
Unit:				
Defining:	Activities: (examples)		Assessment:	Resources: (focus only)
Locating:				
Selecting/Analyzing:				
Organizing/Synthesizing:				
Creating/Presenting:				
Evaluating:				

Embedding Technology in the Information Literacy Process

Problem setting

Task	Strategy	High-Tech Approach	Low-Tech Approach
Create a problem or meaningful context for the content	Use a community service project or a problem created by students or teacher that is relevant to the children's experiences	Use an Internet-based curriculum project as a context	Use the media or children's experiences

Defining the problem

Task	Strategy	High-Tech Approach	Low-Tech Approach
KWL (K=what we know, W=what we want to know, L=what we need to learn) or concept map	Mind maps	Inspiration Claris Works Draw	Blackline master of a concept map
Outline	Outlining	Microsoft Word	Pencil and paper
SWOT (Strengths, Weaknesses, Opportunities, Threats) analysis	Recording	Inspiration Claris Works Word Processing Microsoft Word	Pencil and paper
Brainstorm	Share ideas	e-mail lists discussion boards	Class discussion Multiage projects teams Talk to family at home Cross-class discussions

Locating information

Task	Strategy	High-Tech Approach	Low-Tech Approach
Locate resources	Books, videos, pictures	Automated library	Browsing the local library
Locate resources	CD-ROM searching	Encarta CD Groliers CD World Book CD	Print encyclopedias
Locate resources	Internet searching	AltaVista HotBot	No low-tech alternative
Locate resources	Internet indexes	Yahooligans	No low-tech alternative
Primary sources	E-mail interviews	Microsoft Express E-mail	Personal interviews
Data collection	Experiment	Remote sensing	Hands-on experiments

Embedding Technology in the Information Literacy Process

Selecting/Analyzing

Task	Strategy	High Tech	Low Tech
Recording facts and ideas	Outlining	Microsoft Word Claris Works Word Processing	Pencil and paper 3 X 5 cards
	Note taking	Microsoft Encarta Research Organizer World Book Homework Wizards	Pencil and paper

Organizing/Synthesizing

	Spreadsheet	Claris Works Spreadsheet Microsoft Excel	Y Chart X Chart
	Database	Claris Works Database Microsoft Access	Venn diagrams
	Outline	Claris Works Word Processing	Pencil and paper
	Note taking	World Book	Pencil and paper
	Time lines	Timeline Wizard	

Creating/Presenting

		Microsoft Powerpoint Hyperstudio Kid Pix Studio Claris Works Word Processing Microsoft Publisher HTML Storybook Weaver	Poster Handwritten report Diorama

Evaluating

	Learning log Reflective journal	Microsoft Word Claris Works Word Processing	Handwritten

Name: _____   Date: _____

Analyzing my task — checklist

Check the boxes and fill in as many spaces as you can for your task

What is my task?   _____

_____

_____

* Do I work alone ☐   or in a group? ☐

* Who is my audience? _____   * What will my final product be? e.g., Report _____

* Due date? ___/___/___   * How long do I have to complete this task? _____ weeks.

* What teacher checkpoints do I have? _____

* What do I have to hand in with the final copy?

    Research organizer ☐   Note cards ☐   Draft copy ☐   Bibliography ☐

    Working disk ☐   Other _____

What will my final presentation be?   **oral** ☐   **written** ☐   **visual** ☐

---

oral

    * How long will my talk be? _____ minutes.

    * Will I word process/ write my note cards?

    * What other posters/interesting items/people could I use in my talk?

    _____

---

written

    * What format will I use?

    handwritten ☐   word-processed ☐

    * How long will it be? _____

---

visual

    * What format will I use?

    video ☐   dramatic presentation ☐   multimedia ☐

    poster ☐   model/construction ☐   photo ☐

    other _____

Defining: Analyzes and clarifies requirements of task

Name: _____   Date: _____

Analyzing the task

What exactly am I asked to do?

Key words/phrases relating to Content in the task...

1.

2.

3.

4.

5.

Key words/phrases relating to Processes in the task ...

1.

2.

3.

4.

5.

Task requirements...

*

*

*

*

Defining: Analyzes and clarifies requirements of task

Name: Date:

Analyzing the task

What exactly am I asked to do?

Key words/phrases relating to Content in the task...

TEACHING TIPS...

- ♦ This deconstruction will assist students to focus on the exact requirements of the task.

5

Key words/phrases relating to Processes in the task ...

1.

2.

3.

4.

5.

Defining: Analyzes and clarifies requirements of task

Name: _____   Date: _____

Planning outline

Problem/Task:

Task requirements:

Assessment timeline: **Teacher's signature**

..…/..…/..…   Research notes completed   _____

..…/..…/..…   First draft completed   _____

..…/..…/..…   Teacher/peer conference   _____

..…/..…/..…   Final presentation   _____

Defining: Analyzes and clarifies given task

Name: _____   Date: _____

Planning outline

Problem/Task:

Task requirements:

> ### TEACHING TIPS...
>
> ♦ Use to set assignment tasks. Set task as a problem whenever possible. It is very important that the problem be as relevant to the student as possible in order to enhance student engagement and motivation.
>
> ♦ Information Literacy Skills should be embedded within the Task Requirements.

Assessment timeline:		Teacher's signature
...../...../.....	Research notes completed	
...../...../.....	First draft completed	
...../...../.....	Teacher/peer conference	
...../...../.....	Final presentation	

Defining: Analyzes and clarifies given task

Name: _____   **Date:** _____

Task Sheet

Task: _____

_____

_____

_____

Audience: _____

Final product: _____
(e.g., Persuasive Essay)

Assignment Checkpoints: (e.g., Notes, First Draft, etc.)   **Date**

_____   _____

_____   _____

_____   _____

_____   _____

Final presentation requirements:

Research Organizer   Draft copy   Other _____
Note cards   Working disk

Task Criteria:

*
*
*
*
*
*
*
*
*

Defining: Analyzes and clarifies requirements of task

Name: Date:

Task Sheet

Task: _____

_____

_____

_____

Audience: _____

Final product: _____
(e.g., Persuasive Essay)

TEACHING TIPS...

♦ This sheet has been designed to be used for short tasks.

♦ Ensure that the Set Task description provides students with a clear understanding of the steps involved in completing this task.

♦ Statement of Task should be structured in such a way as to allow students to analyze and make decisions about the relevance of information.

♦ Framing the Question — Assignments or Tasks should be framed in such a way as to avoid a simple `cut and paste' exercise, which is merely the process of reading and regurgitating information, and inevitably results in plagiarism.

♦ Assignments which have relevance to the student — are "real," or as close to real-life as possible — will engage the mind and heart of students and foster a spirit of inquiry and enthusiasm for the task.

♦ It is critical that Assignment Tasks are framed in such a way as to allow the students to give an opinion or create original responses to the problem.

Defining: Analyzes and clarifies requirements of task

Name: Date:

Brainstorming

What do I already know about this problem/task?

Getting started...

Defining: Draws on prior knowledge to brainstorm and cluster ideas

Name: _____ Date: _____

Brainstorming

What do I already know about this problem/task?

_____

_____

_____

_____

Getting started.....

TEACHING TIPS...

• Designed to be a free-thinking activity.   A mind map of vocabulary and prior knowlege is constructed, and links made to associated ideas.

• Transfer brainstorming to concept map to create headings and focus questions.

Defining: Draws on prior knowledge to brainstorm and cluster ideas

Name: Date:

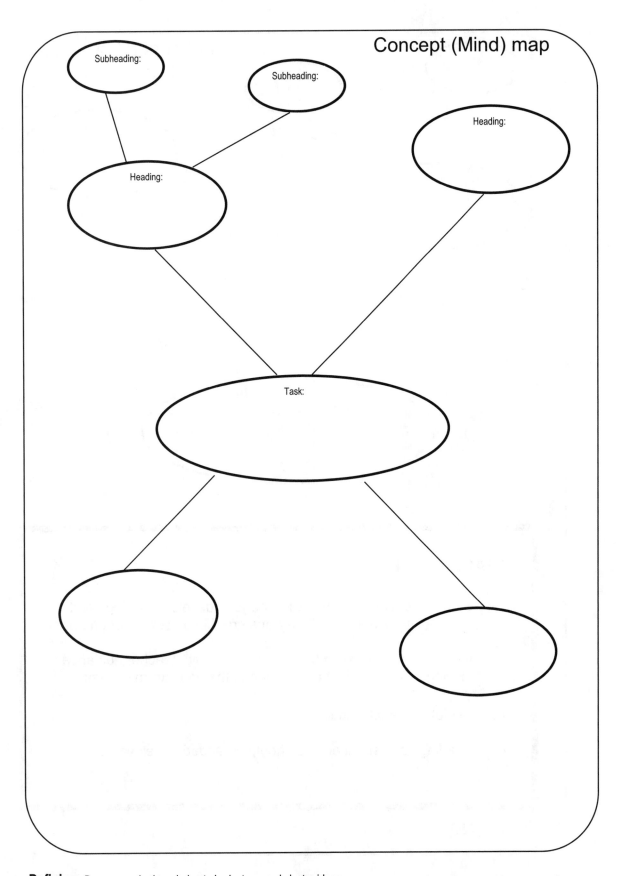

Concept (Mind) map

Subheading:

Subheading:

Heading:

Heading:

Task:

Defining: Draws on prior knowledge to brainstorm and cluster ideas

Name: Date:

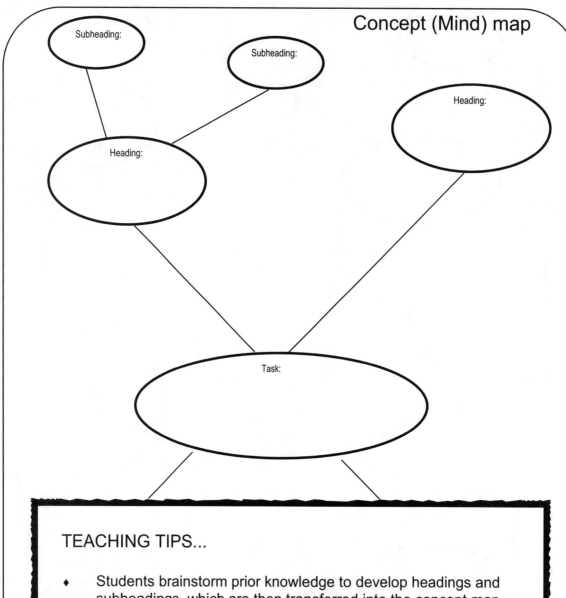

Concept (Mind) map

Subheading:

Subheading:

Heading:

Heading:

Task:

TEACHING TIPS...

♦   Students brainstorm prior knowledge to develop headings and
    subheadings, which are then transferred into the concept map.

♦   Initially, students would brainstorm ideas with teacher guidance,
    moving to independent completion of the brainstorming task.

♦   Useful for visual learners.

♦   Headings and subheadings should be added as relevant.

Defining: Draws on prior knowledge to brainstorm and cluster ideas

Name: _____   Date: _____

Tree Diagram

Task/Problem: _____

_____

Heading: _____

```
                        ┌──────────────────┐
                        │                  │
                        │  _____  │
                        └────────┬─────────┘
          ┌──────────────────────┼──────────────────────┐
  ┌───────────────┐      ┌───────────────┐      ┌───────────────┐
  │               │      │               │      │               │
  │ _____  │      │ _____  │      │ _____  │
  └───────┬───────┘      └───────┼───────┘      └───────┬───────┘
     ┌────┴────┐                 │              ┌────────┴────────┐
  ┌──────┐  ┌──────┐             │          ┌──────┐      ┌──────┐
  │      │  │      │             │          │      │      │      │
  │ ____ │  │ ____ │             │          │ ____ │      │ ____ │
  └──────┘  └──────┘             │          └──────┘      └──────┘
                            ┌────┴────┐
                        ┌──────┐  ┌──────┐
                        │      │  │      │
                        │ ____ │  │ ____ │
                        └──────┘  └──────┘
```

Defining: Draws on prior knowledge to brainstorm and cluster ideas

From *Information Literacy Toolkit,* published by the American Library Association. Copyright © 2001 by Jenny Ryan and Steph Capra. All rights reserved except those which may be granted by Sections 107 and 108 of the Copyright Revision Act of 1976.

Name: _____   Date: _____

Tree Diagram

Task/Problem: _____

_____

Heading: _____

```
              ┌──────────────┐
              │  ─────────── │
              └──────┬───────┘
          ┌──────────┼──────────┐
    ┌───────────┐┌───────────┐┌───────────┐
    │ ───────── ││ ───────── ││ ───────── │
    └─────┬─────┘└─────┬─────┘└─────┬─────┘
      ┌───┴───┐    ┌───┴───┐
   ┌────┐┌────┐ ┌────┐┌────┐
   │    ││    │ │    ││    │
```

TEACHING TIPS...

An alternative framework to a concept map.

♦ Use when brainstorming.

♦ Useful for visual learners.

Defining: Draws on prior knowledge to brainstorm and cluster ideas

Name: Date:

Graphic Outline

Task/Problem: _____

_____

Heading: _____

    Subheading   a] _____

                        b] _____

                        c] _____

Heading 2. _____

    Subheading   a] _____

                        b] _____

                        c] _____

Heading 3. _____

    Subheading   a] _____

                        b] _____

                        c] _____

Heading 4. _____

    Subheading   a] _____

                        b] _____

                        c] _____

Defining: Draws on prior knowledge to brainstorm and cluster ideas

Name: _____   Date: _____

Graphic Outline

Task/Problem: _____

_____

Heading: _____

    Subheading   a] _____

                      b] _____

                      c] _____

Heading 2. _____

    Subheading   a] _____

                      b] _____

                      c] _____

Heading 3. _____

TEACHING TIPS...

- ♦ This Graphic Outline is designed to provide an overview and structure of the task.

- ♦ Use as an overhead transparency for modeled example of note-taking outline.

- ♦ Useful for logical thinkers.

Defining: Draws on prior knowledge to brainstorm and cluster ideas

Name: _____   Date: _____

What do I need to find out? _____
_____

Subheading	Focus question

What resources could I use?

Primary sources of information...

People ☐   Artifact ☐   Field trip ☐

Secondary sources of information...

Book ☐   Encyclopedia ☐   CD-ROM ☐

Video ☐   Audio tape ☐   Internet ☐

Other _____

_____

_____

Defining: Develops focus questions using modeled techniques/Makes predictions about likely sources of information

Name: _____   Date: _____

What do I need to find out? _____

Subheading	Focus question

What resources could I use?

TEACHING TIPS...

♦   Develops Focus questions derived from subheadings.

♦   Focus questions are very important. Properly constructed Focus questions will lead to successful completion of the Assignment Task.

♦   Makes predictions about likely sources of information using this outline.

_____

_____

Defining: Develops focus questions using modeled techniques/Makes predictions about likely sources of information

Name: _____   Date: _____

Task: _____
_____

Subheading	Focus question

Possible sources of information...

Primary sources
Interview/Survey   Document
Field trip   Artifact

Secondary sources
Book   Encyclopedia   CD-ROM
Video   Internet   Journal/Newspaper
Audio tape

Other   _____
               _____

Defining: Develops focus questions using modeled techniques/Makes predictions about likely sources of information

Name: _____ Date: _____

Task: _____

Subheading	Focus question

TEACHING TIPS...

♦ After completing brainstorming task requirements and devising Headings and Subheadings, appropriate Focus questions should be developed to guide the research process.

♦ "Possible sources of information" is a reminder to students to access a variety of resources and to be selective regarding the relevance of resources.

Defining: Develops focus questions using modeled techniques/Makes predictions about likely sources of information

Name: _____   Date: _____

Bookmark

Cut around the outside of the bookmark.
Design and draw your own personal logo for the bottom sections of your bookmark.
Gently score with scissors, or fold, along center line. Glue together.

Problem solving or completing a task	How do I choose a book that's just right for **ME???**
Define the problem... What exactly do I have to do?	
	BLIPA
Locate resources... Where will I find the information I need?	**B]** Read the **BLURB** to see if the book has an interesting story line.
Select/Analyze... Which of these resources will be of use to me?	**L]** Look at the **LENGTH** to see how long it might take to read.
Organize/Synthesize... How can I best organize my information to solve my problem/complete my task?	**I]** Read the **INTRODUCTION** to see how well you can read this particular book.
Create/Present... How can I best present my solution?	**P]** Look at the **PICTURES** and **PRINT** and the size of the type.
Evaluate... How well did I complete my task?	**A]** Ask **ADVICE** from friends, teachers and the library media specialist.
	✓✓✓
Name:	

Defining: Analyzes and clarifies a given task/Assesses readability of materials

Bookmark

Cut around the outside of the bookmark.
Design and draw your own personal logo for the bottom sections of your bookmark.
Gently score with scissors, or fold, along center line. Glue together.

Problem solving or completing a task	How do I choose a book that's just right for **ME???**
Define the problem... What exactly do I have to do?	BLIPA
Locate resources... Where will I find the information I need?	**B]** Read the **BLURB** to see if the book has an interesting story line.
Select/Analyze... Which of these resources will be of use to me?	**L]** Look at the **LENGTH** to see how long it might take to read.
Organize/Synthesize...	**I]** Read the **INTRODUCTION** to see

TEACHING TIPS...

♦ Photocopy onto colored paper to enhance impact of book mark.

♦ When introducing the Assignment Task, revise the steps in the Information Process.

♦ Use the BLIPA technique to guide students in the selection process of Fiction.

Name:	

Defining: Analyzes and clarifies a given task/Assesses readability of materials

Name: Date:

Hypothesis

A hypothesis is the opening statement that outlines your proposed argument. This statement will be proved in your discussion.

Hypothesis: _____

_____

_____

Supporting arguments are taken from the points you outlined in your hypothesis. Each point is developed logically and sequentially to prove your hypothesis.

Supporting arguments (in note form)

Point 1: _____

_____

_____

_____

Point 2: _____

_____

_____

_____

Point 3: _____

_____

_____

_____

Point 4: _____

_____

_____

_____

The Conclusion **MUST RESTATE** the hypothesis, i.e., — The supporting arguments given prove the hypothesis, which is then restated.

Conclusion: _____

_____

_____

_____

Defining: Formulates a basic hypothesis

Hypothesis

A hypothesis is the opening statement that outlines your proposed argument. This statement will be proved in your discussion.

Hypothesis: _____

_____

_____

Supporting arguments are taken from the points you outlined in your hypothesis. Each point is developed logically and sequentially to prove your hypothesis.

Supporting arguments (in note form)

Point 1: _____

_____

_____

_____

Point 2: _____

_____

_____

_____

Point 3: _____

TEACHING TIPS...

♦ Extensive modeling and practice are required for students to acquire the concept of developing a hypothesis. This sheet has been designed to be used as either an introduction or revision to hypotheses.

♦ A hypothesis is integral to a Persuasive Argument, and may be used for an Analytical Essay.

♦ May be used in conjunction with Debates (as a form of Persuasive Argument).

Defining: Formulates a basic hypothesis

Name: _____   Date: _____

Researching from an Internet site

Heading: _____

Focus question: _____

Search terms: _____

Internet icon	* Click on desktop **Browser Icon** - Netscape/Explorer
Search Engine	* Select appropriate **Search Engine**, e.g., Alta Vista.
Search Term/s	* Use **Help Function** to refine search, then use your identified terms to commence search.
Select site/s	* Select the site most likely to contain relevant information. NOTE: It is important to **read descriptions of sites** very carefully to ensure their relevance to your task. * Scroll through web site, scan text and take notes as appropriate.

Key Words	Notes - Information (In point form — list each new idea on a separate line)	Site Address

Locating: Uses special reference tools - Internet sites

Name: _____ Date: _____

Researching from an Internet site

Heading: _____

Focus question: _____

Search terms: _____

(Internet icon) * Click on desktop **Browser Icon** - Netscape/Explorer

(Search Engine) * Select appropriate **Search Engine**, e.g., Alta Vista.

TEACHING TIPS...

♦ Use when introducing students to open Internet searching.

♦ Emphasis should be placed on the importance of using the online help to ensure optimum results from each Search Engine. Students need to be aware that Search Engines do differ in the way searches are made.

♦ Possible search terms should be brainstormed prior to going online to avoid unnecessary waste of time.

♦ Revise use of :
Back button/Arrow;
Side Bar scrolling to move down page;
Hand to indicate Hyperlinks;

♦ Note change of color in hyperlinked text once accessed.

♦ It is very important to **record sources of information** (Site Addresses) **as they are accessed** to avoid having to try to find the same site at a later date.

Locating: Uses special reference tools - Internet sites

Name: _____   Date: _____

Boolean Searching

Inquiry/CD/Internet — Possible Search Terms: _____

_____

The use of **AND** refines the search to include only those subjects in which both terms are present, e.g., Natural disasters AND cyclones (Where circles overlap)

The use of **OR** refines the search to include those subjects in which either term is present, e.g., Natural disasters or cyclones:

The use of **NOT** refines the search to include Natural disasters, but NOT cyclones:

Resources found:

(e.g., Books — Book Title, Dewey No.
          Internet — Internet address;
          CD-ROM — Subject title)

Book Title	Dewey No.	Internet Address	CD-ROM Search Term
_____	_____	_____	_____
_____	_____	_____	_____
_____	_____	_____	_____
_____	_____	_____	_____
_____	_____	_____	_____
_____	_____	_____	_____
_____	_____	_____	_____

Locating: Uses simple and combined terms to search catalog, Internet, CD-ROM.

Boolean Searching

Inquiry/CD/Internet — Possible Search Terms: _____

The use of **AND** refines the search to include only those subjects in which both terms are present, e.g., Natural disasters AND cyclones (Where circles overlap)

TEACHING TIPS...

Students need to check database (catalog, CD-ROM and WWW) for appropriate Search Terms.

♦ Use this worksheet to introduce simple Boolean Searching using AND, OR and NOT searches.

♦ A record of possible resources may be compiled using this sheet.

♦ May be used to assist in the compilation of Bibliography.

Book Title	Dewey No.	Internet Address	CD-ROM Search Term
_____	_____	_____	_____
_____	_____	_____	_____
_____	_____	_____	_____
_____	_____	_____	_____
_____	_____	_____	_____
_____	_____	_____	_____
_____	_____	_____	_____

Locating: Uses simple and combined terms to search catalog, Internet, CD-ROM.

Name: _____   Date: _____

Web Page Review

Responsibility

Author's name: _____

Qualifications: _____

Organization/Association: _____

Date of Publication/Update: _____

Country of origin: _____

Site: Commercial ☐   Education ☐   Organization ☐   Government ☐

Reliability

Bias? (Stereotypes, generalizations, exaggeration). Give example: _____

_____

Verifiable?. Give example: _____

Two other sources supporting similar ideas?: Give example: _____

_____

Current?. Give example: _____

Contact information (e-mail)?   Give address: _____

Relevance

Can you understand the text?	Yes/No
Does the information help to answer your original task?	Yes/No
Is the page layout easy to read?	Yes/No
Is the site easily accessible from the front page?	Yes/No
Does the site have links that are easy to follow?	Yes/No
Do the links take you to relevant information?	Yes/No

Useless   Valuable

Value of this site to my current task?   └────────┴────────┘

Selecting/Analyzing: Analyzes appropriate information from a variety of sources

Name: _____   Date: _____

Web Page Review

Responsibility

Author's name: _____

Qualifications: _____

Organization/Association: _____

Date of Publication/Update: _____

Country of origin: _____

Site: Commercial ☐   Education ☐   Organization ☐   Government ☐

TEACHING TIPS...

Responsibility:

♦ Discuss the issue of lack of authority in many Web sites. How should this be addressed by your students?

♦ Discuss the structure of the address, e.g.,
   org means organization,
   com means commercial and
   edu means educational institution.

♦ Discuss update, and the extent to which the site may have been revised.

Reliability:

It is advisable for students to work with materials from a variety of sources in order to have a general understanding of the topic. It is important to check credentials of Web page authors to verify authenticity, bias and reliability of information.

Relevance to task:

As with any information resource, emphasis should be placed on the importance of remaining focused on the set task.

Selecting/Analyzing: Analyzes appropriate information from a variety of sources

Detecting Bias

Resource review to detect bias

Most authors represent a viewpoint when writing.
It is important to be aware of the point of view when taking notes from different sources.
Point of view may be subtle or obvious.
Obvious point of view becomes bias.

REVIEW

Author: _____

Title: _____

_____

Date of Publication: _____

Qualifications (if any) of author: _____

Membership of organization: _____

Example of vocabulary expressing bias: _____

_____

Example of ideas expressing bias: _____

_____

Facts supported by other writers:

1] _____

2] _____

Overall is this writing biased? (Using the information gained in the previous two points, discuss whether the bias outweighs the supported facts.)

_____

_____

_____

What point of view is the author trying to convey?

_____

_____

Selecting/Analyzing: Identifies strategies used to slant information in subtle ways

Detecting Bias

Resource review to detect bias

Most authors represent a viewpoint when writing.
It is important to be aware of the point of view when taking notes from different sources.
Point of view may be subtle or obvious.
Obvious point of view becomes bias.

REVIEW

Author: _____

Title: _____

_____

Date of Publication: _____

TEACHING TIPS...

♦   Students should be made aware that bias may be identified through establishing the point of view of an organization or an individual, and that what may be seen as bias by one group may be viewed as fact by another.

♦   It is important that the text used as a modeled example of bias is relevant to the current task.

♦   Extensive modeling is required to identify words used to express bias and to locate facts supported by other writers.

♦   A critical aspect of this skill is that the students are led to draw conclusions regarding the extent of bias.

♦   Bias may be detected by observing the author's use of emotive language.

Qualifications (if any) of author: _____

Selecting/Analyzing: Identifies strategies used to slant information in subtle ways

Name: _____　　　　Date: _____

Taking notes from a Speaker

Name of Speaker: _____

Title of talk: _____

_____

a]　_____

　　i]

　　ii]

　　iii]

　　iv]

　　v]

b]　_____

　　i]

　　ii]

　　iii]

　　iv]

　　v]

c]　_____

　　i]

　　ii]

　　iii]

　　iv]

　　v]

d]　_____

　　i]

　　ii]

　　iii]

　　iv]

　　v]

Selecting/Analyzing: Uses a variety of Primary and Secondary sources

Name: _____   Date: _____

Taking notes from a Speaker

Name of Speaker: _____

Title of talk: _____

_____

a] _____

    i]

    ii]

    iii]

    iv]

    v]

b] _____

    i]

    ii]

    iii]

    iv]

    v]

c] _____

    i]

    ii]

    iii]

TEACHING TIPS...

♦ This sheet assists students to organize information in a logical sequence and enables students to identify and summarize the key elements of a presentation by a speaker.

Selecting/Analyzing: Uses a variety of Primary and Secondary sources

Taking notes from a Speaker

Name of Speaker: _____

Title of talk: _____
_____

Theme:

Selecting/Analyzing: Uses a variety of Primary and Secondary sources

Name: _____   Date: _____

| Taking notes from a Speaker |

Name of Speaker: _____

Title of talk: _____
_____

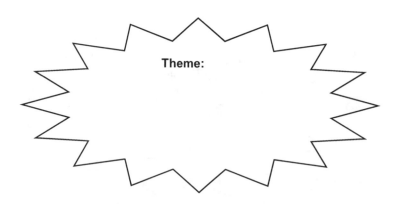

Theme:

TEACHING TIPS...

♦ This sheet is designed to assist students to cluster information in a logical manner.

♦ Visual learners are able to identify and summarize the key elements of a presentation by a speaker.

Selecting/Analyzing: Uses a variety of Primary and Secondary sources

Name: _____ Date: _____

Brief Research Notes

Heading: _____

Focus Question: _____

Key Words	Notes — Information (In point form — list each new idea on a separate line)	Information Source (For Bibliography)

Heading: _____

Focus Question: _____

Key Words	Notes - Information (In point form — list each new idea on a separate line)	Information Source (For Bibliography)

Organizing/Synthesizing: Makes notes using modeled techniques, e.g., written bulleted points

Name: _____   Date: _____

Brief Research Notes		
Heading: _____		
Focus Question: _____		
Key Words	**Notes — Information** (In point form — list each new idea on a separate line)	**Information Source** (For Bibliography)

Heading: _____

TEACHING TIPS...

- Students identify key words within the information text. Notes are then made in point form using own words to express ideas/concepts in text.

- This step is very important in giving students the skills to create their own ideas and not copy those of others.

- Use for headings/subheadings requiring a brief response only.

- These notes are ideal to form the basis of note cards. Construction of note cards requires extensive modeling and guidance — entire presentation SHOULD NOT be written on note cards.

Organizing/Synthesizing: Makes notes using modeled techniques, e.g., written bulleted points

Name: _____   Date: _____

Research notes		
Heading: _____		
Focus Question: _____		

Key word	Notes — Information (In point form — list each new idea on a separate line)	Information Source (For Bibliography)

Organizing/Synthesizing: Makes notes using modeled techniques, eg., written bulleted points

Research notes

Heading: _____

Focus Question: _____

Key word	Notes — Information (In point form — list each new idea on a separate line)	Information Source (For Bibliography)

TEACHING TIPS...

♦ Students identify key words within the information text. Notes are then made in point form using own words to express ideas/concepts in text.

♦ This step is very important in giving students the skills to create their own ideas and not copy those of others.

♦ Use for headings/subheadings requiring detailed response.

♦ These notes are ideal to form the basis of note cards. Construction of note cards requires extensive modeling and guidance — entire presentation SHOULD NOT be written on note cards.

Organizing/Synthesizing: Makes notes using modeled techniques, eg., written bulleted points

Name: _____   Date: _____

Bibliography

Primary sources...

Person/artifact/place:

Who/What/Where	Date	Place

Secondary sources...

Book:

Author	Date	Title	Publisher	Place

Encyclopedia:

Title	Date	Vol No	Page No/s

CD-ROM:

Author	Title	Date	Publisher

Internet:

Author	Title of Entry	http	Date of download

Organizing/Synthesizing: Records bibliographic sources of information using author, title, publisher, date, http, download

Name: Date:

Bibliography

Primary sources...

Person/artifact/place:

Who/What/Where	Date	Place

Secondary sources...

Book:

Author	Date	Title	Publisher	Place

Encyclopedia:

Title	Date	Vol No	Page No/s

TEACHING TIPS...

♦ Students record the bibliographic information as they use each resource.

♦ During the selection process, students would have entered details of all relevant resources on this worksheet. Additional records would be added during the Organizing/Synthesizing phase if needed.

Organizing/Synthesizing: Records bibliographic sources of information using author, title, publisher, date, http, download

Name: _____ Date: _____

Paragaph No: _____ _____

_____

_____

_____

_____

_____

_____

_____

_____

_____

_____

_____

Paragraph No: _____ _____

_____

_____

_____

_____

_____

_____

_____

_____

_____

_____

_____

Organizing/Synthesizing: Categorizes information according to a framework of headings and subheadings

Name: _____   Date: _____

_____

Paragaph No: _____

_____

_____

_____

_____

_____

_____

_____

_____

_____

_____

_____

_____

Paragraph No: _____

TEACHING TIPS...

- Construct cohesive paragraphs using points from Research Notes.

- Paragraphs should directly address Focus Questions.

- Lead Sentences could be developed at this point, i.e., an opening statement that introduces the content of the paragraph.

- This is the beginning of the synthesizing process leading to the development of original ideas in response to the task.

Organizing/Synthesizing: Categorizes information according to a framework of headings and subheadings

Name: _____   Date: _____

Brief Research Notes

Heading: _____

Focus Question: _____

_____

_____

Notes — Information
(In point form — list each new idea on a separate line)

_____

_____

_____

_____

_____

_____

_____

_____

_____

_____

_____

Reference: _____

_____

_____

_____

_____

_____

_____

_____

_____

_____

_____

_____

_____

_____

_____

Reference: _____

Organizing/Synthesizing: Records information using appropriate note-making strategy

Brief Research Notes

Heading: _____

Focus Question: _____

_____

Notes — Information
(In point form — list each new idea on a separate line)

_____

_____

_____

_____

_____

_____

_____

_____

_____

_____

Reference: _____

TEACHING TIPS...

♦ Designed to be used where a brief response is required.

♦ Emphasis should be placed on the importance of recording bibliographic details at the time of using the resource for later inclusion in a full Reference List.

Reference: _____

Organizing/Synthesizing: Records information using appropriate note-making strategy

Name: _____   Date: _____

Research Notes

Heading: _____

Focus Question: _____

_____

Notes — Information

(In point form — list each new idea on a separate line.
References should be recorded after using each resource.)

_____

_____

_____

_____

_____

_____

_____

_____

_____

_____

_____

_____

_____

_____

_____

_____

_____

_____

_____

_____

_____

_____

_____

_____

_____

_____

_____

_____

Reference: _____

Organizing/Synthesizing: Records information using appropriate note-making strategy

Name: _____ Date: _____

Research Notes

Heading: _____

Focus Question: _____

_____

Notes — Information
(In point form — list each new idea on a separate line)
References should be recorded after using each resource.

_____

_____

_____

_____

_____

_____

_____

_____

_____

_____

_____

_____

_____

_____

_____

_____

TEACHING TIPS...

♦ Emphasis should be placed on the importance of recording
    bibliographic details at the time of using the resource for later
    inclusion in a full Reference List.

_____

_____

_____

Reference: _____

Organizing/Synthesizing: Records information using appropriate note making strategy

Name: _____   Date: _____

Draft References

(Replace italics with underlining for handwritten lists)

Primary sources:

Person/artifact/site -   **Note:**   [1]Statement by George Davison, senior citizen, personal interview.
                                        Brownstown, Ohio, July 22, 1998.

                          Reference: Davison, George. Personal interview. Brownstown, Ohio, July 22, 1998.

Person/artifact/site : _____

_____

_____

_____

Secondary sources:

Book: **Single author:** Kennedy, Margaret. *Flowers of the Midwest.* New York: Avon Books, 1995.

          Multiple authors: Adams, Muriel, William Meadows, and Gerald Smith. *School Libraries in an Information Age.* Chicago: Education
                      Press, 1998.

          No author: *Birds in Your Back Yard.* New York: Bird Watchers Society of America, 1990.

Book: _____

_____

_____

_____

_____

_____

_____

Encyclopedia: **Author:** Lee, Matthew. "Penguins," *Encyclopedia Americana,* 1998, xvi, pp. 353-355.

                No author: "Inventions," *World Book Encyclopedia,* 1996, x, pp. 310-332.

Encyclopedia: _____

_____

_____

Magazine/Newspaper article: **Author:** Henderson, Grace. "Has Homework Gotten Out of Hand?" *Tamaroa Times,* August 20, 1999.

                            No author: "Previously Owned Cars," *Automobile Buyer's Guide,* December 1998, pp. 74-77.

Magazine/Newspaper article: _____

_____

_____

_____

Organizing/Synthesizing: Records bibliographic sources of information using author, title, publisher, date, http, download

Draft References

Secondary sources:

CD-ROM: *Guinness Disc of Records.* CD. Britannica Software, 1996.

CD-ROM: _____

_____

_____

_____

Internet: Bruce, Howard. "Documenting Electronic Sources for Your Term Paper," Seven Steps in Writing a Research Paper, April 21, 1999. <www.smla.respap.org>.

Internet: _____

_____

_____

_____

_____

Video: *The Great Barrier Reef.* Videocassette. Goldcrest, 1999.

Video: _____

_____

_____

Sample References (in Alphabetical Order)

Adams, Muriel, William Meadows, and Gerald Smith. *School Libraries in an Information Age.* Chicago: Education Press, 1998.

Birds in Your Back Yard. New York: Bird Watchers Society of America, 1990.

Bruce, Howard. "Documenting Electronic Sources for Your Term Paper," *Seven Steps in Writing a Research Paper,* April 21, 1999. <www.smla.respap.org>

Davison, George. Personal interview. Brownstown, Ohio, July 22, 1998.

The Great Barrier Reef. Videocassette. Goldcrest, 1999.

Guiness Disc of Records. CD. Britannica Software, 1996.

Henderson, Grace, "Has Homework Gotten Out of Hand?" *Tamaroa Times,* August 20, 1999.

"Inventions," *World Book Encyclopedia,* 1996, x, pp. 310-322.

Kennedy, Margaret. *Flowers of the Midwest.* New York: Avon Books, 1995.

Lee, Matthew. "Penguins," Encyclopedia Americana, 1998, xvi, pp. 353-355.

"Previously Owned Cars," *Automobile Buyer's Guide,* December 1998, pp. 74-77.

Organizing/Synthesizing: Records bibliographic sources of information using author, title, publisher, date, http, download

Name: _____   Date: _____

References

Notes: (Include Direct and Indirect References), e.g.,
Direct quote: George Davison said, " ....[1]"
Indirect quote: George Davison (1998) believes that ....

References

Example 1: Davison, George. Personal interview. Brownstown, Ohio, July 22, 1998.

_____

_____

_____

_____

_____

_____

_____

_____

_____

Organizing/Synthesizing: Records bibliographic sources of information

References

Notes: (Include Direct and Indirect References), e.g.,
Direct quote: George Davison said, " .... [1]"
Indirect quote: George Davison (1998) believes that ....

TEACHING TIPS...

♦ There are two main aspects to Referencing an Assignment —

a] Notes are given at the end of the chapter for a quote, (Direct) or as supporting evidence (Indirect).

b] Full details of the References are given at **the end** of the piece of writing.

♦ Referencing shows:
* where the ideas have come from;
* ideas and opinions of others;
* source of facts;
* source of quotes.

Organizing/Synthesizing: Records bibliographic sources of information

Name: _____   Date: _____

| Analyzing a problem... using PMI |

Task/Problem: _____

_____

_____

_____

Plus

*

*

*

*

Minus

*

*

*

*

Interesting

*

*

*

*

Organizing/Synthesizing: Is aware there may be alternative solutions to a problem

Name: _____   Date: _____

Analyzing a problem... using PMI

Task/Problem: _____

_____

_____

_____

Plus

* *
* *
* *
* *

Minus

TEACHING TIPS...

P - **Positive** elements of a discussion
M - **Negative** elements of a discussion
I - **Interesting** aspects of the discussion.

♦ May be used to analyze an issue/situation/organization,
  e.g., Problem: Should we colonize Antarctica?

♦ Information from PMI may be used as basis for class or small group
  discussion and analysis.

Organizing/Synthesizing: Is aware there may be alternative solutions to a problem

Heading: _____

Focus Question: _____
_____
_____

FOR	AGAINST

Organizing/Synthesizing: Compares information from different sources for opposing viewpoints and accuracy

Name: _____   Date: _____

Heading: ————————————————————————————————————

Focus Question: ————————————————————————————

——

——

FOR	AGAINST

TEACHING TIPS...

- Use to assist in the development of an argument, such as Persuasive Essay or Debate — Examine the differing points of view taken from different sources, e.g., foreign troops engaging in peace-keeping roles for civil disputes.

Organizing/Synthesizing: Compares information from different sources for opposing viewpoints and accuracy

Name: _____   Date: _____

Observation Notes: _____

Date	Notes	Diagram

Date	Notes	Diagram

Date	Notes	Diagram

Organizing/Synthesizing: Verifies results of experiments

Name: _____   Date: _____

Observation Notes: _____

Date	Notes	Diagram

Date	Notes	Diagram

TEACHING TIPS...

Designed to be used for:
  Science:
  * observations, recording procedures, experiments

  History:
  * recording historical events, e.g., sequence of events
    leading to Pearl Harbor

  English:
  * plot sequencing

Organizing/Synthesizing: Verifies results of experiments

Name: _____   **Date:** _____

Fact and Opinion

Heading: _____

Focus Question: _____

_____

Source: (Newspaper, Magazine, WWW page, etc.)
Author/Date/Page no/Title/Place/Issue

Source 1: _____

FACT	OPINION

Source 2: _____

FACT	OPINION

Organizing/Synthesizing: Begins to discriminate between fact and opinion

Fact and Opinion

Heading: _____

Focus Question: _____

_____

Source: (Newspaper, Magazine, WWW page, etc.)
Author/Date/Page no./Title/Place/Issue

Source 1: _____

FACT	OPINION

TEACHING TIPS...

♦ Use when introducing students to analysis of text.

♦ Facts identified must be substantiated within the text.

♦ Sources used may contain opposing viewpoints or opinions, or may contain a combination of both fact and opinion.

♦ Record bibliographic details for future reference.

♦ The qualifications/credentials of the author may lend weight to the author's arguments or statements.

Organizing/Synthesizing: Begins to discriminate between fact and opinion

Name: Date:

Research Notes in Tabular Form

Features			Consequences: (if applicable)

Map/Diagram/Sketch

Organizing/Synthesizing: Records information using appropriate note-making strategy

Name: _____   Date: _____

	Research Notes in Tabular Form		
Features	*Country A*	*Country B*	**Consequences** (If applicable)
Population			
G N P			
Literacy level			
Poverty level			

Map/Diagram/Sketch

TEACHING TIPS...

♦ Useful for note-making where comparison is appropriate.

♦ Map/Diagram/Sketch would complement information entered into the table.

Organising/Synthesising: Records information using appropriate note-making strategy

Name: _____   Date: _____

Cause and Effect

Cause   **Effect**

_____   _____
                                       _____
                                       _____

_____   _____
                                       _____
                                       _____

_____   _____
                                       _____
                                       _____

_____   _____
                                       _____
                                       _____

Conclusions: _____
_____
_____
_____
_____
_____
_____
_____
_____
_____

Organizing/Synthesizing: Synthesizes information to predict consequences and to construct generalizations

Name: _____   Date: _____

Cause and Effect

Cause	Effect

TEACHING TIPS...

- Particularly useful for problem-centered tasks or Focus Questions where links from key words in the problem are to be identified.

- A critical aspect of this activity is that the information is analyzed in order for the student to come to a conclusion or solution regarding the original task or problem.

Organizing/Synthesizing: Synthesizes information to predict consequences and to construct generalizations

Name: _____   Date: _____

Sequencing

Task: Explain how... _____

```
┌─────────────┐          ┌─────────────┐
│             │          │             │
│             │          │             │
│             │          │             │
└─────────────┘          └─────────────┘
      ↓                        ↑
┌─────────────┐          ┌─────────────┐
│             │          │             │
│             │          │             │
│             │          │             │
└─────────────┘          └─────────────┘
      ↓                        ↑
┌─────────────┐          ┌─────────────┐
│             │          │             │
│             │          │             │
│             │          │             │
└─────────────┘          └─────────────┘
      ↓                        ↑
┌─────────────┐          ┌─────────────┐
│             │          │             │
│             │     →    │             │
│             │          │             │
└─────────────┘          └─────────────┘
```

Organizing/Synthesizing: Proposes a solution to a set problem which organizes ideas and information logically

Name: _____   Date: _____

Sequencing

Task: Explain how... _____

```
┌─────────────┐        ┌─────────────┐
│             │        │             │
│             │        │             │
│             │        │             │
└─────────────┘        └─────────────┘
      ↓                       ↑
┌─────────────┐        ┌─────────────┐
│             │        │             │
│             │        │             │
│             │        │             │
└─────────────┘        └─────────────┘
```

TEACHING TIPS...

♦ This sheet has been designed to be used for Procedural Tasks, e.g., Explain how a rotary engine works.

♦ Useful for visual learners.

```
┌─────────────┐        ┌─────────────┐
│     ↓       │        │     ↑       │
│             │        │             │
│             │ →      │             │
│             │        │             │
└─────────────┘        └─────────────┘
```

Organizing/Synthesizing: Proposes a solution to a set problem which organizes ideas and information logically

Name: _____   **Date:** _____

	Sequencing

Task: Explain how .... _____

1]

2]

3]

4]

5]

6]

7]

8]

Organizing/Synthesizing: Proposes a solution to a set problem which organizes ideas and information logically

Sequencing

Task: Explain how ... _____

1]

2]

3]

4]

5]

TEACHING TIPS...

♦ This sheet has been designed to be used for Procedural Tasks, e.g., Explain how a rotary engine works.

♦ Useful for logical thinkers.

♦ May be used as an overhead transparency to model sequencing.

Organizing/Synthesizing: Proposes a solution to a set problem which organizes ideas and information logically

Name: Date:

Compare and contrast

Venn Diagram

Different

Same   Same

Note-taking Grid

Features	x:	y:	Consequences (if applicable)

Organizing/Synthesizing: Combines selected information connecting similar ideas

Name: _____   Date: _____

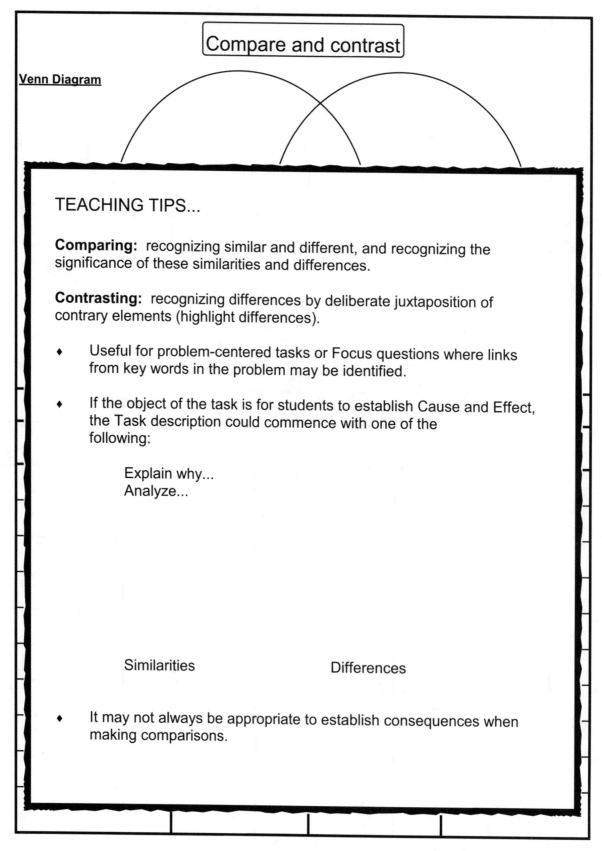

| Compare and contrast |

Venn Diagram

TEACHING TIPS...

Comparing: recognizing similar and different, and recognizing the significance of these similarities and differences.

Contrasting: recognizing differences by deliberate juxtaposition of contrary elements (highlight differences).

♦   Useful for problem-centered tasks or Focus questions where links from key words in the problem may be identified.

♦   If the object of the task is for students to establish Cause and Effect, the Task description could commence with one of the following:

        Explain why...
        Analyze...

Similarities   Differences

♦   It may not always be appropriate to establish consequences when making comparisons.

Organizing/Synthesizing: Combines selected information connecting similar ideas

Name: _____   Date: _____

Debate Organizer

Debate Question: _____

Viewpoint: Affirmative ☐   Negative ☐

Speaker: First ☐   Second ☐   Third ☐

<u>Supporting arguments</u>

First speaker: _____
Argument 1: _____
_____

Argument 2: _____
_____

Second speaker: _____
Argument 1: _____
_____

Argument 2: _____
_____

Third speaker: _____
Argument 1: _____
_____

Argument 2: _____
_____

Note: Use Research Notes sheet for note-taking to elaborate on research arguments.
Possible Rebuttal Points:
1. _____
_____
2. _____
_____

Creating/Presenting: Presents a solution to a problem — debates an issue

Name: _____   Date: _____

Debate Organizer

Debate Question: _____

Viewpoint: Affirmative ☐   Negative ☐

Speaker: First ☐   Second ☐   Third ☐

Supporting arguments

First speaker: _____
Argument 1: _____

_____

Argument 2: _____

_____

Second speaker: _____
Argument 1: _____

_____

Argument 2: _____

_____

TEACHING TIPS...

- Use for introduction to debate planning.

- Use for individual students within the debating teams. Each student completes an individual Debating Organizer noting the points of argument of team members, as well as their own arguments. This will ensure continuity of planning for the debating team.

- Note cards should be made using arguments from the Organizer.

Creating/Presenting: Presents a solution to a problem — debates an issue

Name: Date:

Planning an Oral Presentation

Planning:

    Who is my audience?
    What's my purpose in giving this presentation?

Designing:

    Is my information clear and logically organized?
    Have I supported my ideas with sound reasons?
    What props could I use to make my presentation more interesting?
    Would posters, models, diagrams, exhibits enhance my presentation?
    Do my note cards contain relevant points only?
    Are my note cards clearly written/typed in a large font?

Presenting:

    ✓   DON'T READ my note cards.
    ✓   Keep my head up and look at my audience.
    ✓   Use gestures to emphasize what I'm saying.
    ✓   Try to vary my voice — volume and pace.
    ✓   Speak loudly enough for the people at the back to hear clearly.
    ✓   Make sure I refer to my exhibits at the appropriate time.

Outline for: _____

Introduction: _____

    Point 1: _____

    Point 2: _____

    Point 3: _____

Conclusion: _____

Creating/Presenting: Presents a solution to a problem using an oral presentation

Name: _____   Date: _____

Planning an Oral Presentation

Planning:

Who is my audience?
What's my purpose in giving this presentation?

Designing:

Is my information clear and logically organized?
Have I supported my ideas with sound reasons?
What props could I use to make my presentation more interesting?
Would posters, models, diagrams, exhibits enhance my presentation?
Do my note cards contain relevant points only?
Are my note cards clearly written/typed in a large font?

Presenting:

✓   DON'T READ my note cards.
✓   Keep my head up and look at my audience.
✓   Use gestures to emphasize what I'm saying.
✓   Try to vary my voice — volume and pace.
✓   Speak loudly enough for the people at the back to hear clearly.
✓   Make sure I refer to my exhibits at the appropriate time.

TEACHING TIPS...

◆   Use to guide construction of oral presentations.

◆   Importance of completing the Information Process and of thorough planning of a presentation should be stressed.

◆   Notes taken during the research phase are ideal to form the basis of note cards.

◆   Construction of note cards requires extensive modeling and guidance. Students should not be permitted to read from note cards.

Creating/Presenting: Presents a solution to a problem using an oral presentation

Name: Date:

Planning a Video Presentation

Title: _____

Duration: _____

AUDIO (Music, Voiceover, Dialogue of script)	**VISUAL** (Graphics, Sound effects, description of shots)

Creating/Presenting: Creates a solution to a problem using a video presentation

Name: _____   Date: _____

Planning a Video Presentation

Title: _____

Duration: _____

AUDIO (Music, Voiceover, Dialogue of script)	VISUAL (Graphics, Sound effects, description of shots)

TEACHING TIPS...

♦ Designed to be used to plan the shooting, audio and sequencing of a video production.

♦ Use of this planner minimizes editing sequences of footage.

♦ Voiceover (narration) and dialogue should be scripted in full.

Creating/Presenting: Creates a solution to a problem using a video presentation.

Drawing conclusions

Steps in synthesizing the task...

Task: _____

_____

Heading 1: _____

_____

_____

Heading 2: _____

_____

_____

_____

Heading 3: _____

_____

_____

_____

Heading 4: _____

_____

_____

_____

Heading 5: _____

_____

_____

_____

Heading 6: _____

_____

_____

_____

Creating/Presenting: Presents a solution to a problem which makes simple generalizations and draws simple conclusions

Name: _____ Date: _____

Drawing conclusions

Steps in synthesizing the task....

Task: _____
_____

Heading 1: _____
_____
_____
_____

Heading 2: _____
_____
_____
_____

Heading 3: _____
_____
_____

TEACHING TIPS...

♦ Particularly useful for problem-centered tasks or Focus Questions where links from key words in the problem are to be identified.

♦ Insert Headings as used in Research Notes

♦ For each Heading, summarize the Main Point made by this/these author/s.

NOTE: This is an important step in modeling the synthesizing phase of the Process. Should be used prior to the "Making Connections" Worksheet.

Creating/Presenting: Presents a solution to a problem which makes simple generalizations and draws simple conclusions

Name: _____ Date: _____

Making connections

Steps in synthesizing the task ...

Create your own solutions... ◯

◯ **Plan your course of action...**

Link your information... ◯

Creating/Presenting: Presents a solution to a problem which makes simple generalizations and draws simple conclusions

Name: _____ Date: _____

Making connections

Steps in synthesizing the task ...

TEACHING TIPS...

♦ This is a critical component of the Information Process. It is vital that students synthesize their new information and make links to their existing prior knowledge. This new knowledge then enables them to develop original thoughts and ideas and create original solutions to the set task.

NOTE: It is crucial that the task be set in such a way as to provide the opportunity for students to develop these original thoughts and solutions to problems. Without the opportunity for the inclusion of their own ideas, students are merely being taught to READ and REGURGITATE information, and **plagiarism** is being encouraged.

Create your own solution ...

Plan your course of action...

Creating/Presenting: Presents a solution to a problem which makes simple generalizations and draws simple conclusions

Name: Date:

Self-assessment for group work

How well did I ...   Not at all   Very well

Offer ideas?

Listen to others' ideas?

Value the opinions of others?

Take turns?

Offer to help with difficult tasks?

Remain on task?

Complete my share of the task?

Complete my tasks on time?

Take on a leadership role when necessary?

Help others in the group when appropriate?

I could be a better group member next time by ⎯⎯⎯⎯⎯⎯⎯⎯⎯⎯

Evaluating: Assesses own participation in group

Name: _____   Date: _____

SELF ASSESSMENT

Key: B: Basic; **D:** Developing; **P: P**roficient

Defining:

Overall I have:
- ♦ analyzed and clarified my task

☐

- ♦ constructed appropriate headings and subheadings

☐

Comment:: _____
_____
_____
_____

Locating:

Overall I have:
- ♦ located resources appropriate to my problem/task

☐

Comment:: _____
_____
_____

Selecting/Analyzing:

Overall I have:
- ♦ recorded bibliographic sources of information correctly

☐

- ♦ shown that I have used resources appropriate
   to my problem/task

☐

Comment:: _____
_____
_____
_____

Organizing/Synthesizing

Overall I have:
- ♦ completed an appropriate search strategy plan

☐

- ♦ organized my notes in a meaningful way

☐

- ♦ used adequate and relevant information

☐

- ♦ used appropriate vocabulary

☐

- ♦ used correct spelling and grammar

☐

Comment:: _____
_____
_____
_____
_____

Creating/Presenting:

Overall I have:
- ♦ created a presentation that is logical and well organized

☐

- ♦ shown that I have completed the task requirements

☐

- ♦ created a presentation containing original ideas

☐

Comment: _____
_____
_____

Evaluating: Identifies skills that require practice and refinement/Acknowledges personal achievements

Name: _____   Date: _____

| Reflective Journal |

Date: _____

Comment: (felt, thought, liked/disliked) _____
_____
_____
_____

Date: _____

Comment: _____
_____
_____
_____

Date: _____

Comment: _____
_____
_____
_____

Date: _____

Comment: _____
_____
_____
_____

Date: _____

Comment: _____
_____
_____
_____

Date: _____

Comment: _____
_____
_____

Evaluating: Reflects on personal participation in the process

Name: _____   Date: _____

| Reflective Journal |

Date: _____

Comment: (felt, thought, liked/disliked) _____

_____

_____

_____

Date: _____

Comment: _____

_____

_____

_____

TEACHING TIPS...

♦   Use to focus on the affective domain.

♦   Students reflect on their response/feelings relating to the problem
      or task.

♦   Assists in developing diary writing techniques.

Date: _____

Comment: _____

_____

_____

Evaluating: Reflects on personal participation in the process

Name: _____   Date: _____

SELF ASSESSMENT

Defining
Overall I have: Basic   Proficient
- analyzed and clarified the task requirements
- constructed appropriate headings and subheadings
- followed a time-management strategy to meet given
  dead-lines

Locating
Overall I have:
- located resources appropriate to my problem/task
  from a variety of sources

Selecting/Analysing
Overall I have:
- recorded Bibliographic sources of information correctly
- recorded Reference list of sources correctly
- selected and analyzed resources appropriate to my
  problem/task
- observed copyright conventions

Organizing/Synthesizing
Overall I have:
- made effective use of a search strategy, e.g.,
  Research Organizer
- constructed useful notes
- used adequate and relevant information
- used the appropriate text type structure effectively
- used appropriate vocabulary
- used correct spelling and grammar
- synthesized the new information
- observed ethical guidelines while completing this task

Creating/Presenting:
Overall I have:
- created a presentation that is logical and well organized
- completed the task requirements
- created a presentation containing original ideas
- created a presentation appropriate to my audience

Evaluating
- created a presentation appropriate to my audience

Evaluating: Evaluates understanding and implementation of set task criteria

ASSESSMENT CRITERIA

Student outcomes

Defining:

Overall you have:

Achievement   Effort

- analyzed and clarified your task ☐ ☐

- constructed appropriate headings and subheadings ☐ ☐

Teacher comment: _____

_____

_____

_____

Locating:

Overall you have:
- located resources relevant to your problem/task ☐ ☐

Teacher comment: _____

_____

_____

_____

Selecting/Analyzing:

Overall you have:
- recorded bibliographic sources of information correctly ☐ ☐

- shown that you have used resources appropriate to your problem/task ☐ ☐

Teacher comment: _____

_____

_____

Evaluating: Evaluates understanding and implementation of the set task criteria

Name: _____   Date: _____

ASSESSMENT CRITERIA

> **Key: E:** Excellent; **S:** Satisfactory; **N:** Needs attention

Student outcomes

Organizing/Synthesizing
Overall you have:

	Achievement	Effort
◆ completed a search strategy plan	☐	☐
◆ organized your notes in a meaningful way	☐	☐
◆ used adequate and relevant information	☐	☐
◆ used appropriate vocabulary	☐	☐
◆ used correct spelling and grammar	☐	☐

Teacher comment: _____
_____
_____

Creating/Presenting:

Overall you have:

◆ created a presentation that is logical and well organized	☐	☐
◆ shown that you have completed the task requirements	☐	☐
◆ created a presentation containing original ideas	☐	☐

Teacher comment: _____
_____

Evaluating:
Overall you have:

◆ acknowledged your personal achievements	☐	☐
◆ identified skills that require practice and refinement	☐	☐

Teacher comment: _____
_____

Evaluating: Evaluates implementation and understanding of the set task criteria

Name: _____   Date: _____

ASSESSMENT CRITERIA

Key: E: Excellent; S: Satisfactory; N: Needs attention

Student outcomes

Defining:

Overall you have:
- ♦ analyzed and clarified requirements of the task
- ♦ prepared a relevant and effective search plan

☐ ☐

☐ ☐

Teacher comment: _____

_____

_____

Locating:

Overall you have:
- ♦ shown evidence of adequate and appropriate resource selection

☐ ☐

Teacher comment: _____

_____

_____

Selecting/Analyzing:

Overall you have:
- ♦ recorded bibliographic sources of information correctly
- ♦ shown evidence of critical use of resources
- ♦ shown evidence of critical interpretation and analysis of information

☐ ☐

☐ ☐

☐ ☐

Teacher comment: _____

_____

_____

_____

Evaluating: Evaluates understanding and implementation of set task criteria

Name: Date:

ASSESSMENT CRITERIA

Key: E: Excellent;   **S: S**atisfactory;   **N: N**eeds attention

Student outcomes

Organizing/Synthesizing:

Overall you have:

	Achievement	Effort
◆ completed a search strategy plan	☐	☐
◆ organized your notes in a meaningful way	☐	☐
◆ ensured accuracy of content	☐	☐
◆ ensured adequate and relevant content	☐	☐
◆ used appropriate vocabulary	☐	☐
◆ used correct spelling and grammar	☐	☐

Teacher comment: _____

_____

Creating/Presenting:

Overall you have:

	Achievement	Effort
◆ created a presentation containing original thoughts/solutions	☐	☐
◆ created a presentation that exhibits clarity, accuracy and fluency of expression	☐	☐
◆ ensured that the design/presentation enhances the impact of the presentation	☐	☐
◆ completed the task requirements	☐	☐

Teacher comment: _____

_____

Evaluating:

Overall you have:

◆ acknowledged your personal achievements	☐	☐
◆ identified skills that require practice and refinement	☐	☐

Teacher comment: _____

Evaluating: Evaluates understanding and implementation of set task criteria

Name: _____   Date: _____

Task Assessment Record

Task: _____

Class/Group: _____ **Date:** _____

Key: E: Excellent S: Satisfactory N: Needs attention **Name**	Defining	Locating	Selecting/Analyzing	Organizing/Synthesizing	Creating/Presenting	Evaluating	**Comments**

Name: _____ **Date:** _____

Task Assessment Record

Task: _____

Class/Group: _____ **Date:** _____

Key: **E:** Excellent
S: Satisfactory
N: Needs attention

Name	Defining	Locating	Selecting/Analyzing	Organizing/Synthesizing	Creating/Presenting	Evaluating	Comments

TEACHING TIPS...

♦ The use of an overall rating for each Process simplifies record keeping, yet provides an overview of each student's competencies for that Process. May also be useful in identifying areas of need in a class group.

♦ This sheet is designed to be used in conjunction with other Curriculum Assessment Records by class/subject teachers to monitor progress of individual student's understanding and implementation of the Information Process.

♦ Rating Assessment used is a suggestion only — alternative ratings could be:

B: Basic; **D:** Developing; **P:** Proficient.

Glossary

Compare Look for similarities between the items mentioned.

Contrast Look for differences between the items mentioned.

Criticize Make a judgment about the item in question. Stress the deficiencies.

Define Give a concise and accurate definition

Describe Mention the main characteristics of a situation or retell the main features of a story.

Diagram Provide a drawing, chart or plan.

Discuss Analyze and give reasons for and against and offer an opinion.

Evaluate Give both positive and negative sides of the topic.

Explain Give reasons for what is asked. Provide the causes. For example, explain the reasons for the greenhouse effect.

Illustrate Use examples, or where appropriate provide a diagram or figure.

Interpret Translate, solve, or comment on a subject, usually giving your judgment about it.

Justify Provide the reasons for your conclusions or for the statement made in the question.

List Provide the reasons for your conclusions or for the statement made in the question.

Outline Organize your answer into the main headings and subheadings.

Prove Provide factual evidence, or where appropriate, a logical or mathematical proof.

Relate Show the connection between the items mentioned in the question.

Summarize Provide a summary, usually without comment or criticism.

Trace Describe the progress of some historical event or, where it is appropriate, describe the causes of some event.

Contents

JENNY RYAN has worked in school libraries as a teaching/library professional since 1980. She co-authored *Information Literacy Planning Overview—ILPO* in 1998 with Steph Capra. In 1999, this work was awarded the IASL/SIRS Commendation for innovative practice in school libraries. Ryan has since written several more books and produced a video and other support materials on information literacy with Capra. She currently consults in education, writing and speaking, particularly in the areas of information literacy and information technology.

STEPH CAPRA is currently privately consulting for Capra Ryan & Associates, based in Brisbane, Australia. She has presented workshops and papers in Australia and internationally on issues relating to information literacy and information technology. She has been a professional teacher-librarian for over twenty years. Capra co-authored *Information Literacy Planning Overview—ILPO* with Jenny Ryan in 1998 and has been writing support materials since that time.

The enclosed CD-ROM includes Microsoft Excel® (v 3.0) files prepared by the authors for your use. These files are saved in Macintosh and Windows versions. The electronic files correspond to printed forms in parts 1 and 2 of the text. To open a file, place the CD-ROM in your computer and then browse the CD-ROM for the file you want to use. Copy the file to your hard drive where it can be opened and modified. Each file name ends in the page number where it first appears in the text. For example **(your CD drive letter):\Windows\K-6\Grade 1 Planning Organizer-23.xls** is a Microsoft Excel® for Windows file that is printed on page 23 of *Information Literacy Toolkit: Grades Kindergarten–6*.

For help using the forms and for copyright information please consult the introduction beginning on page ix of this book. For help using Microsoft Excel® please consult your manual or the Microsoft website at www.microsoft.com.

License Restrictions

You may not and you may not permit others to use the software in any manner that infringes the intellectual property or other rights of the authors or another party.

Limited Warranty and Limitation of Liability

For a period of 60 days from the date the Software is acquired by you, the Publisher warrants that the physical media upon which the Software resides will be free of defects that would prevent you from loading the software on your computer. The Publisher's sole obligation under this warranty is to replace defective media, provided you have notified the Publisher of the defect within such 60-day period.

The software is licensed to you "AS-IS" without warranty of any kind. THE PUBLISHER DISCLAIMS ALL OTHER WARRANTIES, EITHER EXPRESSED OR IMPLIED, INCLUDING, BUT NOT LIMITED TO THE IMPLIED WARRANTIES OF MERCHANTABILITY AND FITNESS FOR A PARTICULAR PURPOSE. THE PUBLISHER WILL NOT BE LIABLE FOR DIRECT, INDIRECT, OR CONSEQUENTIAL DAMAGES ARISING OUT OF OR RESULTING FROM YOUR POSSESSION OR USE OF THE SOFTWARE. SOME STATES DO NOT ALLOW THE EXCLUSION OF IMPLIED WARRANTIES, SO THE ABOVE LIMITATIONS OR EXCLUSIONS MAY NOT APPLY TO YOU. THIS WARRANTY GIVES YOU SPECIFIC LEGAL RIGHTS AND YOU MAY ALSO HAVE OTHER RIGHTS WHICH MAY VARY FROM STATE TO STATE.